PULLED THREAD EMBROIDERY

Moyra McNeill

DOVER PUBLICATIONS, INC.
New York

Copyright

Bibliographical Note

This Dover edition, first published in 1993, is an unabridged republication of t‖
paperback edition of *Pulled Thread,* published by Bell & Hyman Limited, London,
1986. The book was originally published by Mills & Boon Limited, Richmond, Surre‖
in 1971.

Library of Congress Cataloging-in-Publication Data

McNeill, Moyra.
   [Pulled thread]
   Pulled thread embroidery / Moyra McNeill.
      p. cm.
   Reprint. Originally published under title: Pulled thread. London : Bell & Hym‖
1986.
   Includes bibliographical references.
   ISBN-13: 978-0-486-27857-5
   ISBN-10: 0-486-27857-3
      1. Drawn-work. I. Title.

TT785.M27   1993
746'.44—dc20

                                                                                              93-329‖
                                                                                                    C

Manufactured in the United States by Courier Corporation
27857306
www.doverpublications.com

Acknowledgements

I am sincerely grateful to the following:

the Whitworth Art Gallery, University of Manchester, the Liverpool City Museums, Gawthorpe Hall, the Embroiderers Guild, and the Victoria and Albert Museum, who have all been most helpful in allowing their collections to be studied;

the Royal School of Needlework and in particular the members of the class in Autumn 1969 for allowing their work to be photographed;

Miss M Forbes, Mrs. Alison Barrell and students of the Textile Group of Beckenham and Penge Adult Education Centre for their generous help and for allowing their work to be borrowed and photographed;

Miss Crawshaw and girls of Great Yarmouth Technical High School;

all those people who contributed information and ideas.

I would also like to thank the many people who most kindly lent their work to be photographed but which for technical reasons it was not possible to include in this book.

CONTENTS

CONTENTS

WHAT IS PULLED THREAD?

Many people are deterred from trying some forms of embroidery simply because their names imply that they are complicated and difficult to learn. There is also a certain mystique about methods like pulled work because some teachers in the past have bounded the technique with rules and strictures which in turn have suggested difficulties that do not exist. It is true that there are one or two extremely complicated stitches which do require concentration, but the aim of this book is to prove how much can be achieved with a basically simple technique, although for those people who wish to go further the challenge of more complex ideas is also presented.

Pulled work and drawn fabric are synonymous, but as drawn fabric can so easily be confused with drawn thread work, pulled thread seems the clearer title. In pulled thread work the threads of the ground material are compressed by pulling stitches tightly, thus forming patterns of holes, and in drawn thread work threads are actually removed from the ground material, usually before any stitching is begun; so although the finished effects of the two methods are vaguely similar the methods are quite different in execution.

Pulled work is also a part of 'linen embroidery', which is a term used by Women's Institutes for a variety of techniques worked on linen.

The use of stitch tension is the main principle that must be understood, as this is the basis of all pulled work. The simplest way to begin is to work a row of satin stitch over four threads, first slackly and then pulling as tightly as possible on the thread. The contrast of effect will be quite obvious. By using this contrast of tension throughout a range of stitches, both rich and lacy textures will be produced, each forming a foil for the other and thus being shown to their best advantage.

An explanation of texture is relevant here: texture is not an abstract term but applies to the surface that is presented to the eye and touch; texture surrounds us in everyday life in walls, floors, clothing, furniture, pavements, roads, grass and plants, and these present surfaces that can be read as smooth, rough, even, shiny, ribbed and so on. If our environment is made up of only one texture it soon becomes boring – for example, rows of brick houses in repetitive streets – but by contrasting brick with trees, grass and paved areas a textural contrast is achieved which is more pleasant simply because it is more varied, and the same general principle applies to the use of texture in much craft work.

A misconception is that pulled work can only be white or beige; this is not true as colour can be used, but after experiment the author has come to the conclusion that pulled work is essentially a monochrome method, as the tightly tensioned stitches are ugly in themselves and it is only when they are completely integrated with the ground material, producing patterns of holes, that they look attractive. Therefore it is quite possible to use rich and bright colours with matching threads, and these can immediately give a more modern effect to a method which has a staid and frumpish image; white can be used effectively on any pale colour as the tone contrast is insufficient to allow any tensioned stitches to show.

Another misconception is that pulled work is essentially very fine and trying to the eyes; while fine work is beautiful, equally effective work can be produced on surprisingly coarse materials and will take a great deal less time.

Nowadays in shops it is possible to see fabrics that have been woven by machine with a texture closely resembling counted thread embroidery. By embroidering all over material repetitively it is possible to produce a very similar effect, which is quite pointless as this by-the-yard look nullifies craftsmanship. The whole point of hand crafts is that they should show individuality and thoughtfulness in design.

There are always people who are naturally attracted by any work on the counted thread, but with the modern, less inhibited approach many other needlewomen may now find this kind of embroidery within their interest and scope.

MATERIALS AND THREADS

Today we have a vast selection of materials and threads to choose from, but as many of the traditional materials and threads go out of production, we are put on our mettle to select the right material for the method. The availability of materials varies from month to month, so that to suggest any one material by name would appear to be pointless, and therefore this chapter will deal with materials in general terms.

For pulled work the fabric must be evenly woven, that is, having the same number of threads per inch or centimetre in warp and weft, and be slightly open in weave, because too close a weave will only cause the material to pucker when pulled stitches are worked on it. The more open the weave the lacier will be the effect, but the most openly woven fabrics have the drawback that they are not suitable for articles to be regularly laundered as the threads can be easily displaced.

For a beginner the best idea would be to write to or visit a reputable supplier of embroidery materials and ask for samples of suitable materials from which a selection can be made, choosing one whose threads can be seen comfortably without strain. Today there is a reasonable range of both white and coloured even-weave linens and cottons, from fairly fine to quite coarse; one point to watch is that coloured fabrics

have not been vat-dyed, as this can mean that the
colour has not fully penetrated the yarn and white
flecks show when threads are pulled aside with
stitchery.

Once some experience has been gained, materials can
be selected from furnishing or dress fabric counters;
curtaining materials of synthetic fibres can often be
found with an even weave, of exciting colour and of
sufficient width to make table linen; some dress linens
can be suitable for pulled work, but synthetics are best
worked in a frame so that the maximum tension can be
exerted on their frequently springy fibres.

Two cheap materials that are particularly useful are
scrim, sold for window cleaning, and dishcloth cotton.
Dishcloth cotton has a particularly open weave and is
best used when learning, or experimentally.

As a general guide the following may be helpful:

Linen
Even weave available from specialist embroidery
suppliers in colours or white (expensive). Scrim for
window cleaning; mid-brown but can be bleached or
dyed (inexpensive). Dress linens by careful selection.

Cotton
Even weave available from specialist embroidery
suppliers in white or colours (reasonably priced).
Dishcloth cotton; cream in colour but can be dyed
(inexpensive).
White canvas; available from art needlework shops for
experimental pulled thread (reasonably priced).

Synthetic fibres
Furnishing fabrics in a variety of colours, widths and
prices.
Curtaining sheers; wide.

14

Wool
Woollen fabrics can sometimes be found with even
weaves but are often closely woven so that the fibres do
not lend themselves to pulled work.

THREADS
A twisted linen embroidery thread is often difficult to
obtain, as it must be strong enough to withstand a
considerable strain. The following is a list of
possibilities which will require experiment by the
worker to find which suits her purpose:
Clark's extra strong button thread.
Coats' extra strong thread (6).
Buttonhole twist.
Crochet threads from fine (80) to thick.
Range of colours in *coton à broder* (18) and a variety of
sizes in white.
Pearl cotton, from thick (3) through sizes 5, 8, to 12
(finest).
Lace threads.
Fine string.

The following may be used in desperation where no
other thread is available, but with the tension required
in this method they either break or go fuzzy and should
therefore be used in short lengths only:
Anchor linen embroidery thread.
Sylko (40).
Stranded cotton.

By experiment it may be found that an unravelled warp
thread of the ground material will be strong enough to
embroider with, a solution that saves both time and
energy.

To match thread and material, it is possible to dye

15

threads and material together if the directions for dyes sold in ordinary hardware shops are followed explicitly, or experiments could be made with natural dyes like onion skins. While it is annoying that a prolonged search for materials inevitably precedes any form of imaginative embroidery, it does ensure a lively approach to their selection which may well prevent a stagnation of ideas and in fact lead to new trains of thought and development which would not otherwise have occurred.

STITCHES

On the following pages are given a variety of stitches
which, when worked, display a range of textures,
beginning with simple forms of counted satin stitch,
and growing increasingly more difficult technically. If
you are a beginner, work chronologically through the
stitches, and when you have finished you will have a
sampler showing the texture of each stitch and will also
have discovered which stitches are most enjoyable to
work and look at.

TECHNICAL HINTS
Needles
Always use tapestry needles for pulled stitches as the
blunt point will not split the threads of the fabric.

Framing
So that threads of the ground material may be more
easily counted, the fabric may be mounted in either
square or circular frames, which may also save having
to stretch the embroidery when completed. Keep the
material really taut in the frame; this will mean
retensioning the material frequently if working on a
piece over a length of time.

To begin a thread there are two ways
Either begin by darning in the thread where it will be
covered with stitchery, taking a back stitch to secure it,
or leave a 3″ (8 cm) end which can be darned into the

back of the stitchery when it is completed. Darn the ends in immediately, as a forest of ends on the back can only be a nuisance.

To end
Darn into the back of the stitchery as invisibly as possible, taking a small back stitch to secure it.

Counting diagonally
Most people find it confusing to count diagonally across threads, so that if it is necessary to count, for example, 4 threads diagonally, count across 4, then down or up 4.

Long jumps across back of work
These are to be avoided where practicable as they may either snag in laundering or show through on the right side. If a long jump is unavoidable, darn the thread under or through a thread of the ground material about every $\frac{1}{4}''$ (6 mm) on the wrong side.

Turning
When it is necessary to come up in the same hole in which the previous row finished, take a small stitch over one thread about three threads away from the hole to secure it; do not pull tightly.

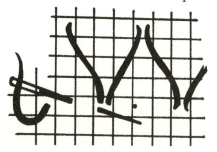

About the photographs in this chapter
The samples have been worked on a bold material and
have been slightly enlarged so that each stitch is visible.
The effect of the stitchery can be altered considerably
by varying the weight and scale of the material; very
fine open materials will produce a lace-like effect and
more closely woven materials a more restrained texture.

About the diagrams
On the graph paper each line represents a thread of
material and each square the space in between the
threads. Dotted lines show where the thread lies on the
wrong side. Each stitch is shown over a specific number
of threads but this may need to be varied depending
on the scale of the material in use. Try a little of each
stitch on an odd piece of fabric before working it *in
situ* to make sure the scale is right.

* indicates that a slack tension should be used, that is,
do not pull the thread at all.
** indicates that medium tension should be applied
with enough pressure to compress and distort the
threads of the ground material.
*** indicates that a really tight tension should be
applied, pulling on the thread as hard as possible, and
needs very strong thread.

Thickness of thread
As a general rule the thread used for pulled work
should be the thickness of a thread from the ground
material. Untensioned satin stitch requires a thicker
thread.

STITCHES BASED ON SATIN STITCH

A great range of stitches are based on satin stitch worked straight on the thread of the material or diagonally. The stitch may be left loose or pulled tight depending on the effect required. Satin stitch on the counted thread is worked between each thread of the ground material.

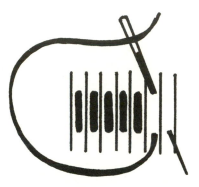

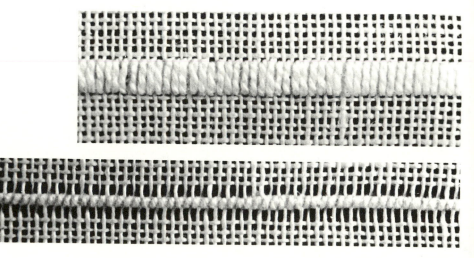

These examples clearly show the effect of tension. The wide stitch was worked over 4 threads slackly * and the narrow one also over 4 threads but tightly ***.

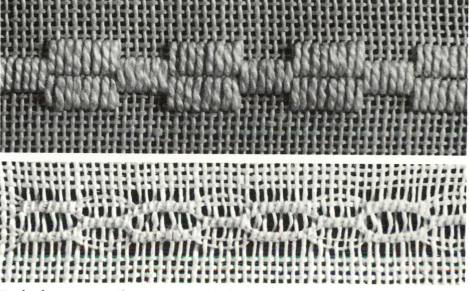

Both these examples were worked in blocks over 4 threads but one * and the other *** with quite different finished results.

The three lines of stitching here show variations in tension.

Top: 10 * stitches, then 3 *** stitches.
Middle: Alternately 8 * and 8 *** stitches.
Bottom: Stitches worked * or *** at random.

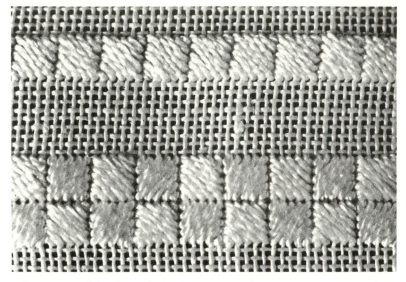

Above are blocks worked diagonally over 1, 2, 3, 4, 5, 4, 3, 2, 1 threads to form a continuous line, and then as a double row slanting in opposing directions *.

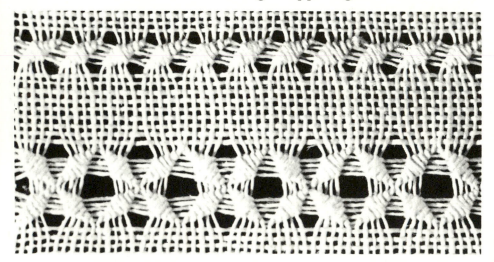

By tightening the tension to *** quite a different effect is achieved. In order to see the threads clearly work in a frame with the material stretched tautly.

Rows of satin stitching combined to form simple
borders that could be made any width.

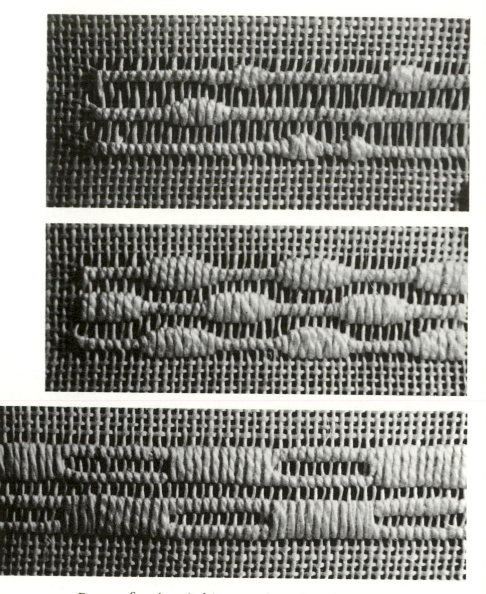

Rows of satin stitching combined to form simple borders that could be made any width.

FILLINGS BASED ON SATIN STITCH
Unless otherwise stated stitches are worked between each thread of the ground material.

Chessboard filling
Blocks of 3 rows of 10 stitches over 3 threads worked in opposing directions; either * or ***.

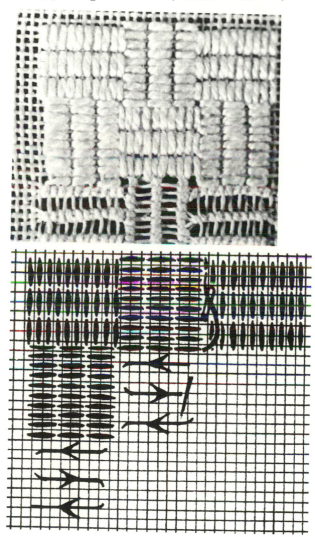

25

Small chessboard filling
Blocks of 2 rows of 7 stitches over 3 threads, in opposing directions; either * or ***.

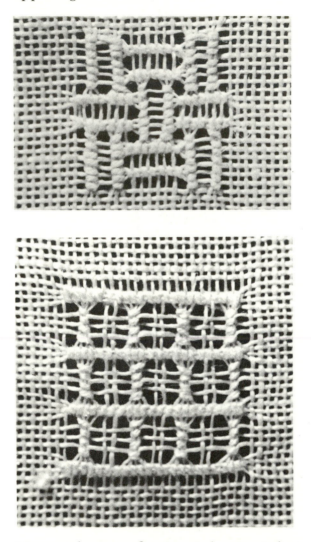

First work rows of satin stitch over 4 threads leaving 3 threads between rows; then work 4 stitches at right angles leaving 2 threads between each (***).

Work blocks of 5 stitches over 4 threads leaving 6
threads in between, overlapping the blocks by 1 thread
(* or ***).

Triangles based on straight stitches over 2, 4, 6, 8
threads, worked in rows diagonally (*).

27

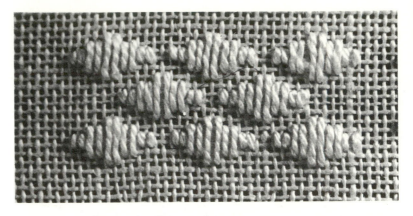

Diamonds formed of 2 stitches over 2, 4, 6, 4, 2 threads, worked in rows leaving 2 threads in between (*).

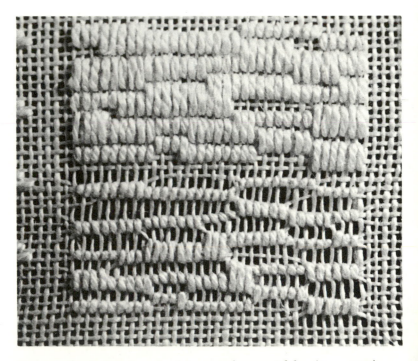

Rows of stitches worked in random widths (* or ***).

Step stitch
Worked diagonally; blocks of 5 stitches over 4 threads at right angles to each other.

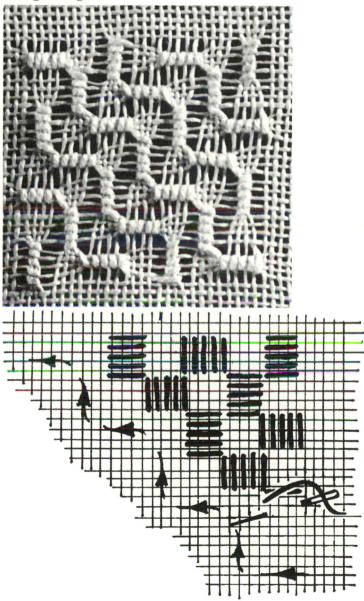

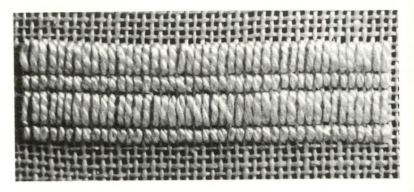

Alternating rows over 4 and 2 threads.

Basket filling is similar to step stitch in movement.

Blocks of 6 stitches over 3 threads are worked at right angles to each other in diagonal rows.

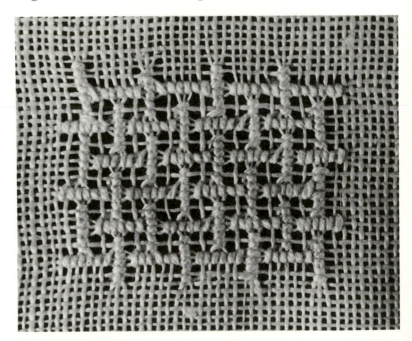

SPACED SATIN STITCH FILLINGS

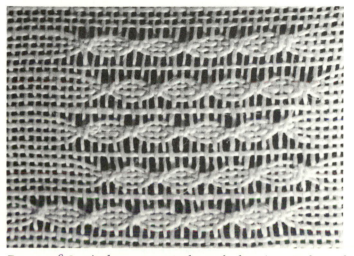

Rows of 2 stitches over 4 threads leaving 5 threads in between; 1 thread left between the rows (**).

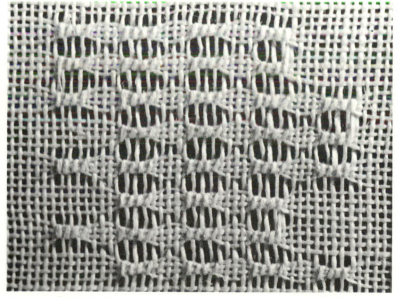

Rows of 4 stitches over 4 threads with 5 threads in between (**).

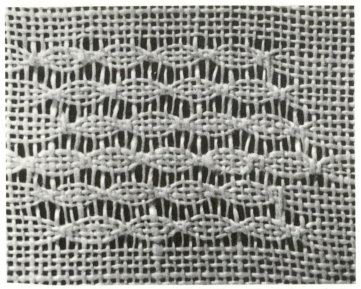

Lines of 2 stitches over 4 threads with 6 threads in between; each line begins 2 threads higher than the previous one (**).

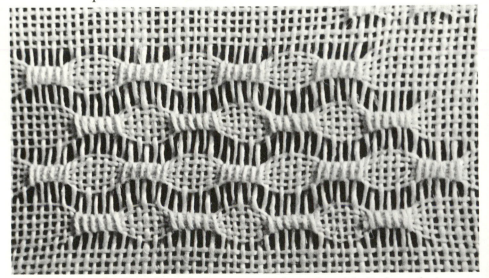

Blocks of 6 stitches over 6 threads with 7 threads in between. Rows bricked (**).

32

Cobbler filling is not as difficult as it looks. Work 1 stitch over 4 threads, leave 2 threads, 1 stitch over 4 threads, leave 4 threads, and repeat to end of row. Work all rows in one direction first, then repeat the rows at right angles (***).

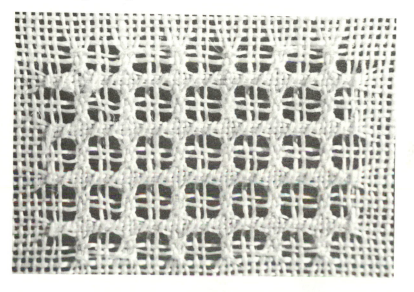

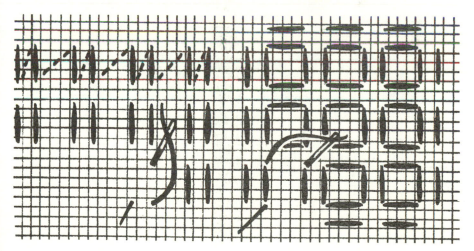

Framed cross filling is worked in the same way as cobbler filling but over a different number of threads, which can be counted from the diagram (***).

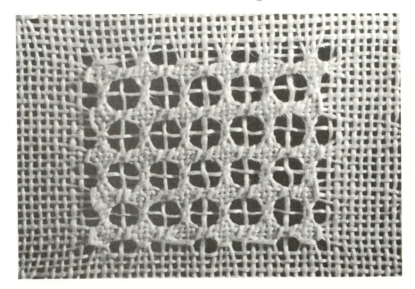

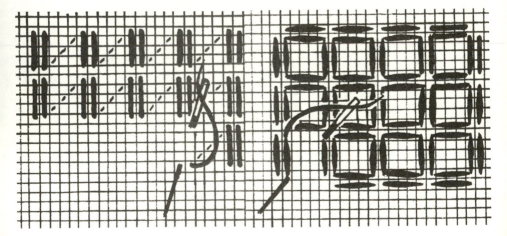

Mock faggot filling

Work 2 stitches over the same 4 threads, leave 4
threads and repeat to form a row. Work all the rows in
one direction, then link up by repeating rows at right
angles using the same holes.

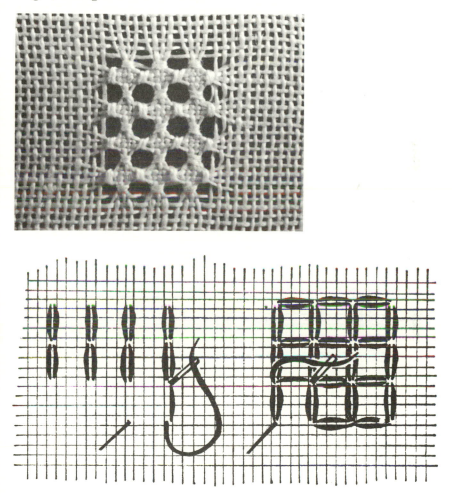

EYELETS

Eyelets are a form of satin stitch, but all the stitches converge on a common centre hole or holes. Bring the needle up on the outer edge and down through the centre for all forms of this stitch because this pulls the centre hole larger. Because of the number of stitches through one hole it is sometimes necessary to use a rather thin thread.

Square eyelet as shown is worked over a square of 8 threads. Begin in the middle of one side by taking a straight stitch over 4 threads and work into each thread round the outer square until the shape is complete (** or ***).

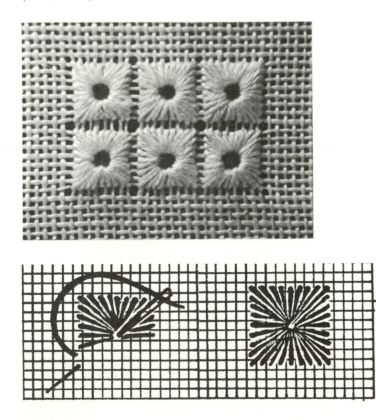

Small eyelet

Work as for square eyelet but only over 2 threads from the centre (** or ***).

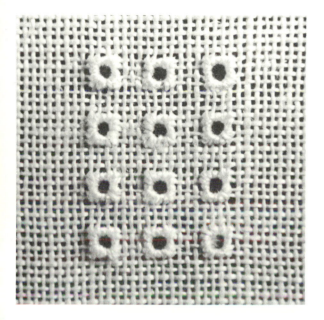

Single cross eyelet

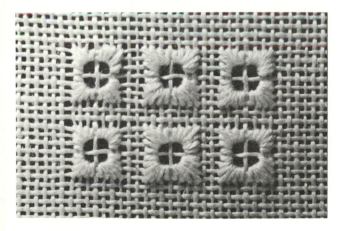

Leave 1 thread between each quarter of a square eyelet (** or ***).

Double cross eyelet
Leave 2 threads between each quarter of a square eyelet and insert a stitch between the 2 threads (** or ***).

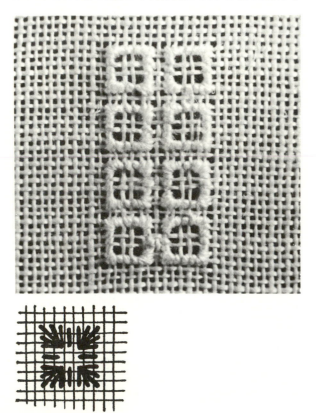

Star eyelet consists of 8 stitches from a central point, one to each corner, and one to the centre of each side, working round the square as for square eyelet. To make a filling, work in diagonal rows (**).

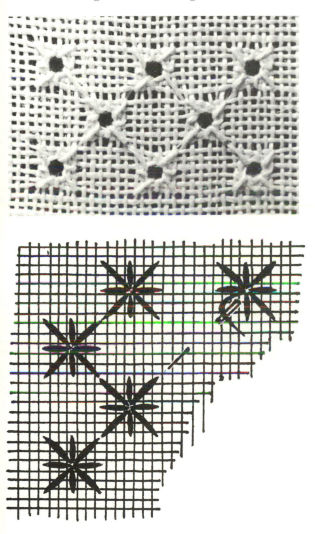

Round eyelet
Work round shapes as in other eyelets but count threads from diagram (**).

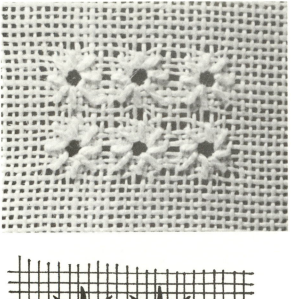

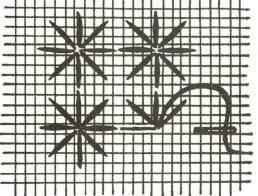

Hexagonal eyelet

Follow diagram for number of threads to go over and work 2 stitches into each hole. Work eyelets in diagonal rows to make a filling (***).

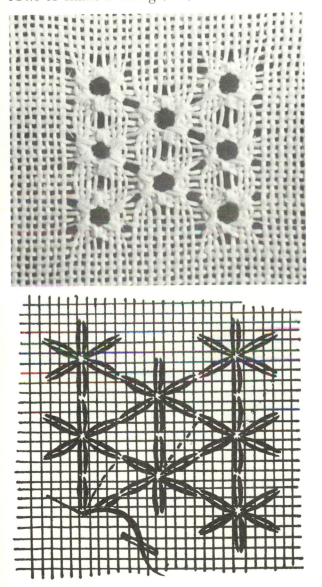

Diamond eyelet

Visualise a diamond shape 10 threads long and wide, and work round shape stitching into each diagonal hole (* or ***).

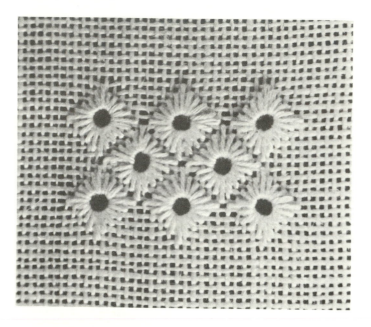

Free eyelets

An interesting and rich texture can be made giving a modern broken effect by working parts of eyelets or moving the hole to one side, and grouping them together (** or ***).

STITCHES BASED ON BACK STITCH
These stitches are all based on back stitch pulled tightly and each stitch is worked over twice.

Pulled back stitch is here worked over 3 threads.

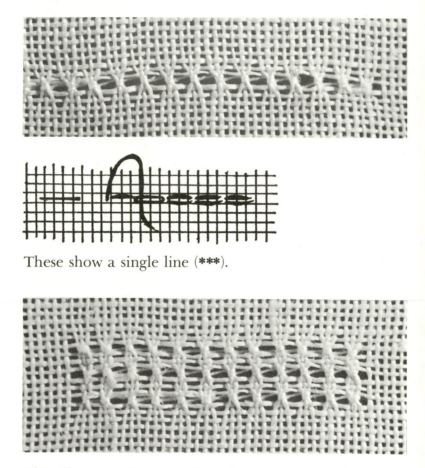

These show a single line (***).

This illustrates 3 rows with 3 threads between the rows (***).

44

Festoon stitch is pulled back stitch in scalloped rows which can be followed from the diagram (***).

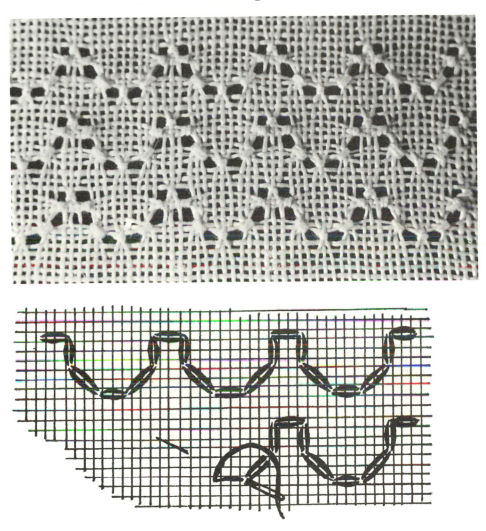

Ringed back stitch is precisely what its name suggests but is worked in a figure-eight movement (see diagram) and where the rows overlap on the return journey 4 stitches will use the same holes (***).

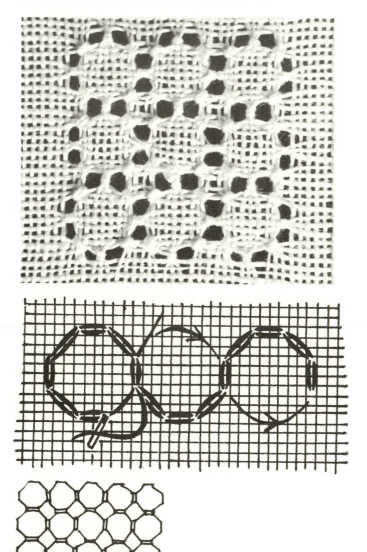

Frost stitch was invented by a student making an error
when learning ringed back stitch, and thereby making
an oval form. It may be worked in a figure eight or
two rows (***).

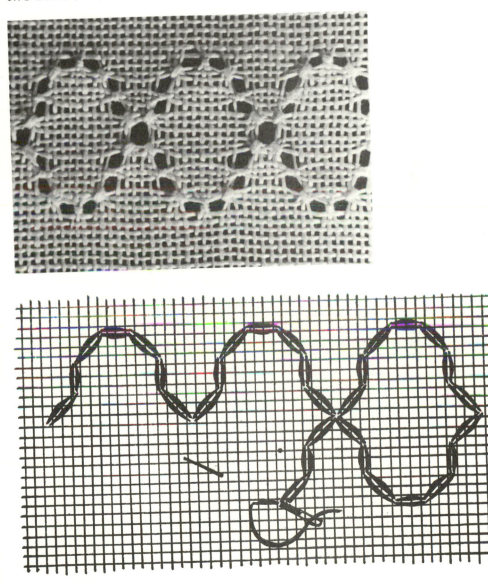

Small ringed back stitch

Having worked the previous stitches the diagram is
self-explanatory. Worked in two rows (***).

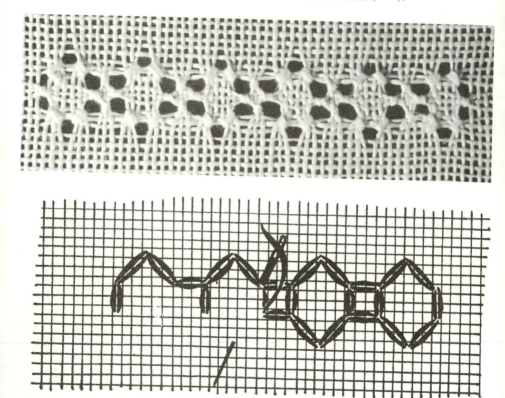

STITCHES BASED ON WAVE STITCH

Wave stitch

Although the stitches appear straight on the fabric when worked, they begin at an angle as can be seen from the diagram, and tight tension pulls them straight. Must be worked over even numbers of threads (***).

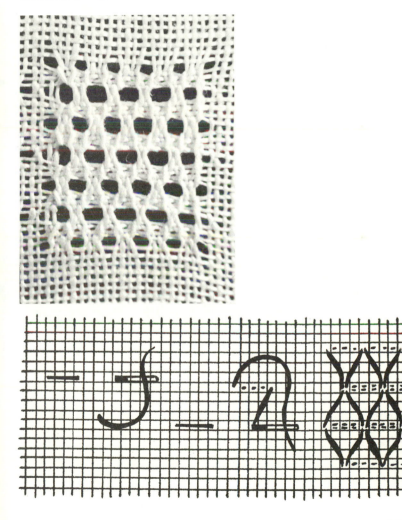

Reverse wave stitch

This stitch is exactly the same as wave stitch,
only the wrong side becomes the right side (***).

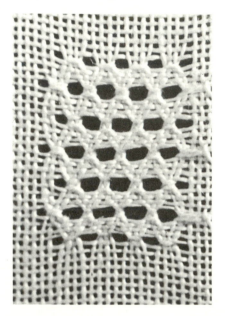

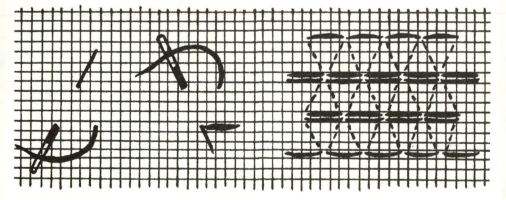

Double wave stitch

Each wave stitch is sewn over twice, giving a bolder effect than wave stitch (***).

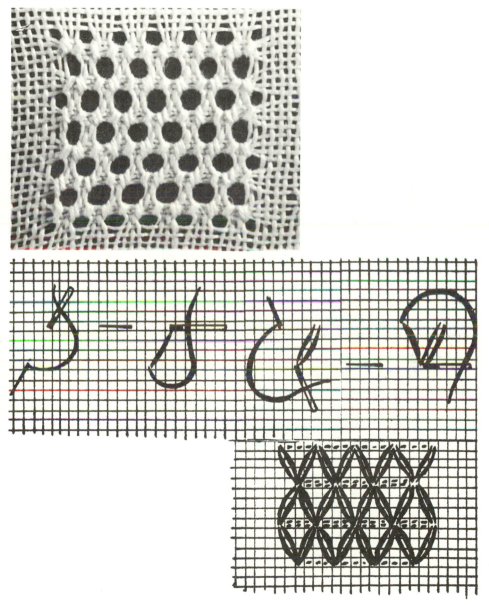

Window filling

This is a wave stitch worked over an uneven number of threads so that a single thread is left between the stitches, which forms the cross in the filling (***).

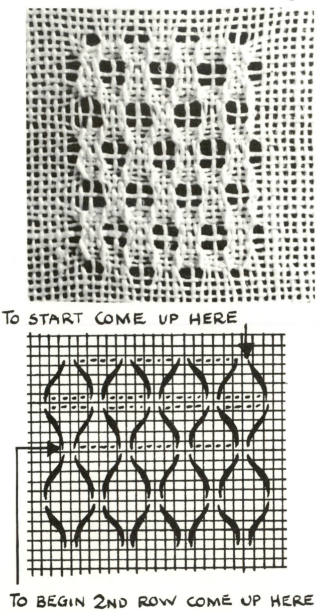

TO START COME UP HERE

TO BEGIN 2ND ROW COME UP HERE

Double stitch filling

This stitch is the reverse side of window filling and
can be made one thread shallower in each row (***).

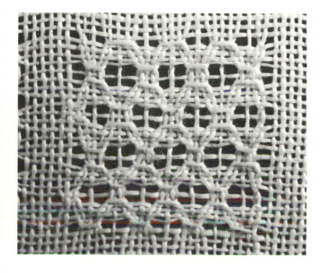

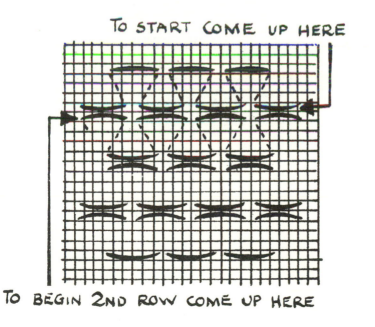

TO START COME UP HERE

TO BEGIN 2ND ROW COME UP HERE

Double window filling is a version of window filling where 2 threads are left between each stitch to form a grid (***).

BEGIN HERE

BEGIN 2ND ROW HERE

Waffle stitch has the same movement as wave stitch except that each stitch begins by being vertical and is slanted with tension (***).

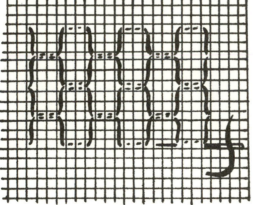

Honeycomb stitch is the same as waffle stitch except that a back stitch is taken over the horizontal threads. Best worked in a heavy thread (*******).

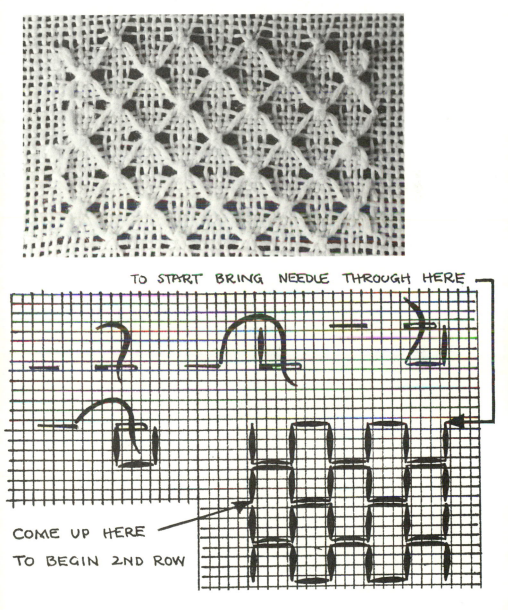

TO START BRING NEEDLE THROUGH HERE

COME UP HERE
TO BEGIN 2ND ROW

Cable stitch is a flattened version of reversed wave stitch; best worked in a thickish thread (**).

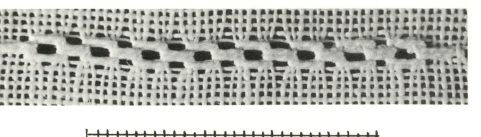

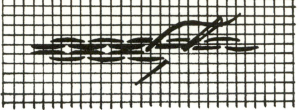

Pebble filling is also a version of reversed wave stitch except that a return row is worked over the spaces in the first row (**).

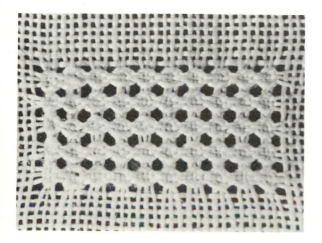

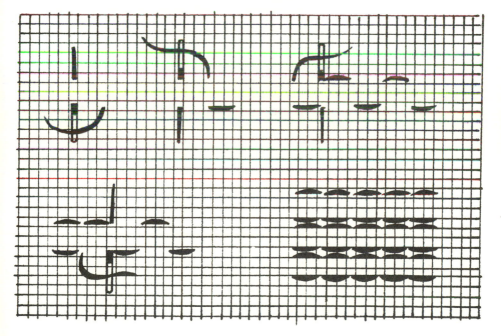

STITCHES BASED ON THE DIAGONAL

Although these stitches are effective on most materials, they may pucker the fabric unless it is loosely woven.

Single faggot stitch

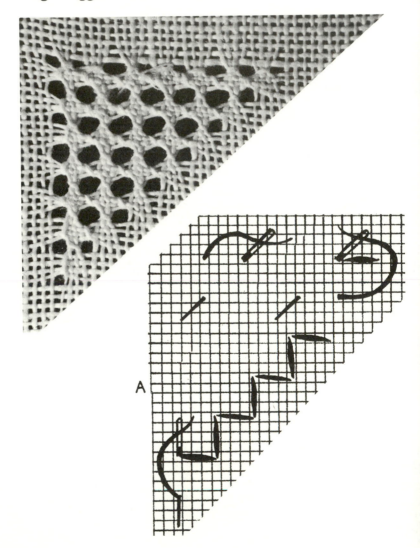

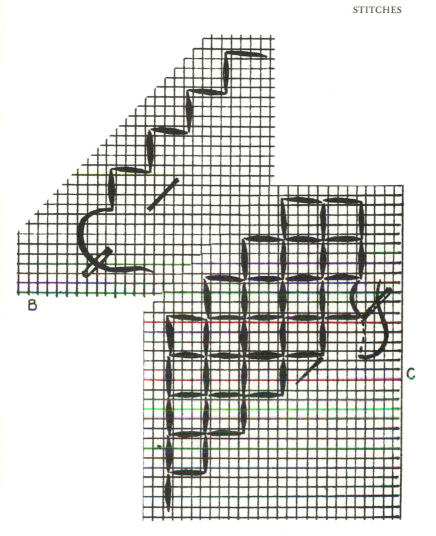

On the right side the stitches are straight on the fabric, and diagonal on the wrong side. 'A' shows the two movements of the stitch and 'B' how to turn. 'C' illustrates several rows of the stitch (*******).

Reverse faggot is precisely what its name suggests and is the reverse side of single faggot (***).

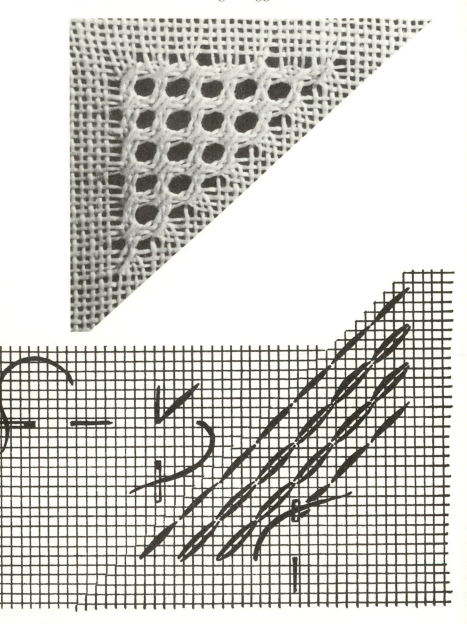

Diagonal drawn filling is single faggot stitch with a
spacing of 1 thread between the rows (***).

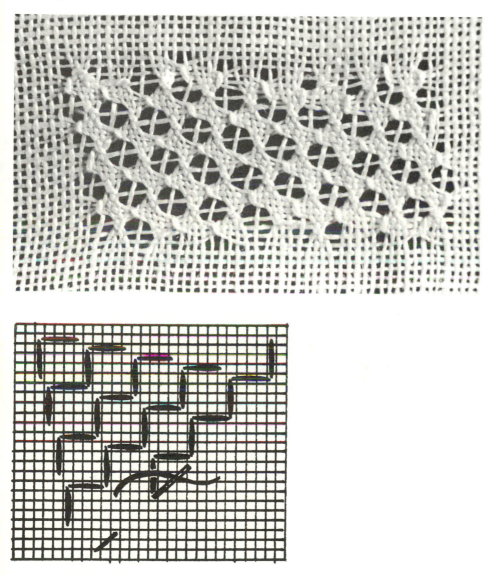

Mixed faggot stitch (diagonal chevron filling) consists of alternate rows of single faggot stitch and reverse faggot stitch. Most effective when worked in a thickish thread, particularly the rows of reverse faggot (*******).

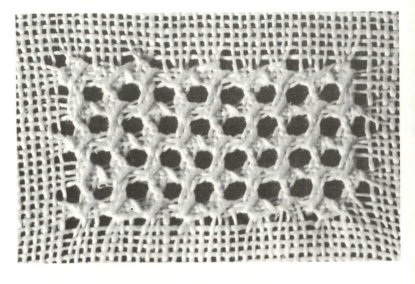

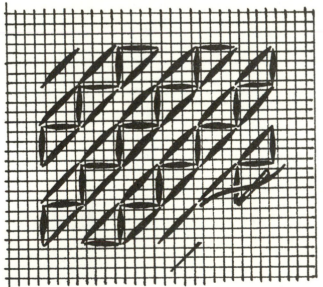

Drawn faggot filling (sometimes known as net filling). Although the diagram seems to have little relation to the photograph, this is how the stitch is worked. A large single faggot over 4 threads alternating with two rows of spaced single faggot over 2 threads (***).

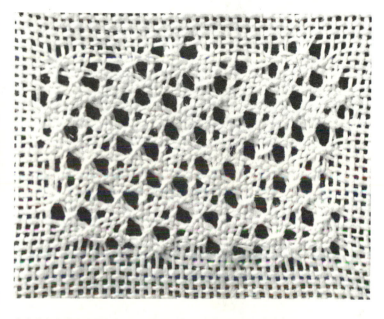

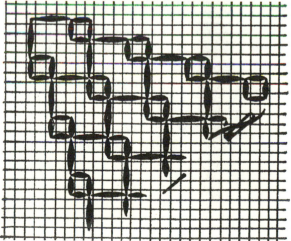

Double faggot is the same as single faggot except that each stitch is worked over twice. When finished it looks almost identical to a fine Russian drawn ground (***).

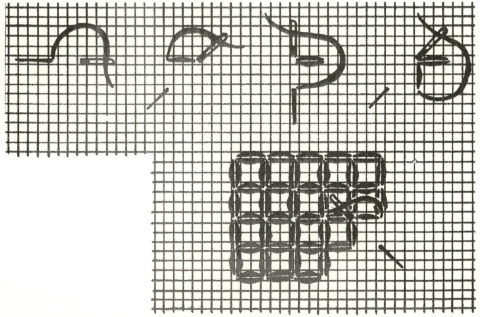

Diagonal cross filling is exactly what its name implies, but work all the half crosses in one row before coming back to complete the crosses. The rows are worked closely together (***).

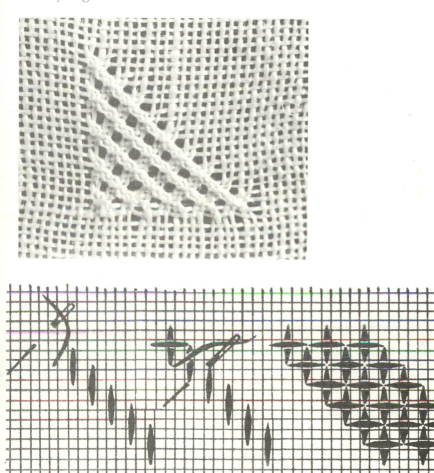

Diagonal raised band is worked in the same way as diagonal cross except the rows are spaced as in the diagram (***).

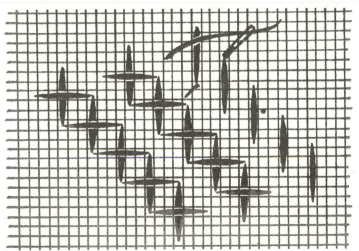

Open trellis filling

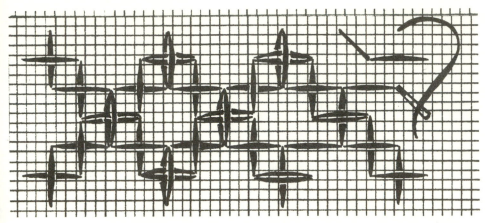

This stitch is another variation of diagonal cross filling.
It begins by being rows of diagonal crosses spaced as
in diagram on previous page. When they are complete,
work the same stitch slanting the other way and
crossing the existing stitches (✱✱✱).

Detached square filling is the reverse side of open trellis
filling (✱✱✱).

Crossed faggot filling

Work single faggot first and then work diagonal cross filling over it in thick thread (***).

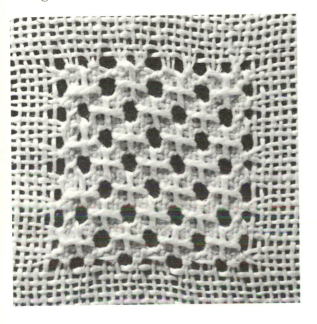

Chequer filling is similar to open trellis filling in that it is basically rows of cross stitch worked diagonally one way, then crossed by rows in the opposing direction. The lower diagram indicates the correct spacing (***).

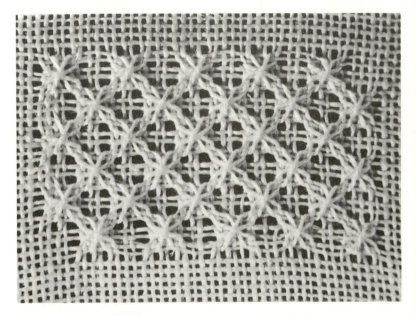

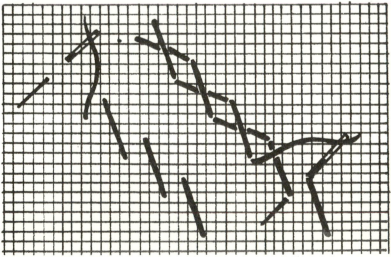

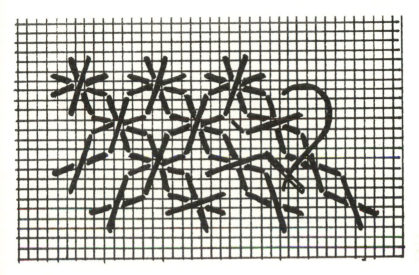

STITCHES BASED ON DOUBLE BACK STITCH

The following stitches are all variations of double back stitch. One form of double back stitch can be worked freely on fine transparent materials when it is called 'shadow work', and on the wrong side it is closed herringbone stitch, so that it is extremely versatile. All these stitches are effective when worked on a loosely woven material because otherwise they can pucker the fabric. To see the threads clearly, double back stitch is best worked in a frame.

Basic double back stitch

Ripple stitch

BEGIN ROW BY COMING UP HERE

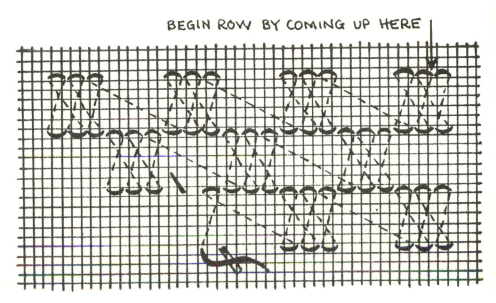

This consists of alternate blocks of double back stitch and spaces, which are in bricked rows to form a filling. A long thread stretches from block to block on the wrong side, which can be lightly darned into the material if this stitch is used on a practical article (**).

Finnish stitch consists of blocks of double back stitch worked in stepped rows as in the diagram (***).

BEGIN ROW BY COMING UP HERE

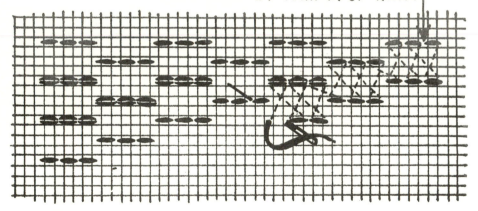

Cushion stitch is formed from rows of oval blocks as shown, and takes its name from the tightly pulled ovals which look padded when worked (***).

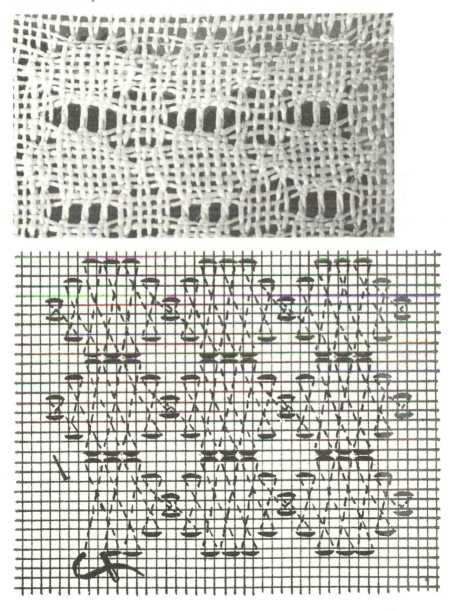

Diamond stitch needs a larger area in which to look its best, and consists of undulating lines worked over the same number of threads throughout. Once the stitch has been learnt, it is possible to vary the size of the diamonds by making the undulations shorter or longer (***).

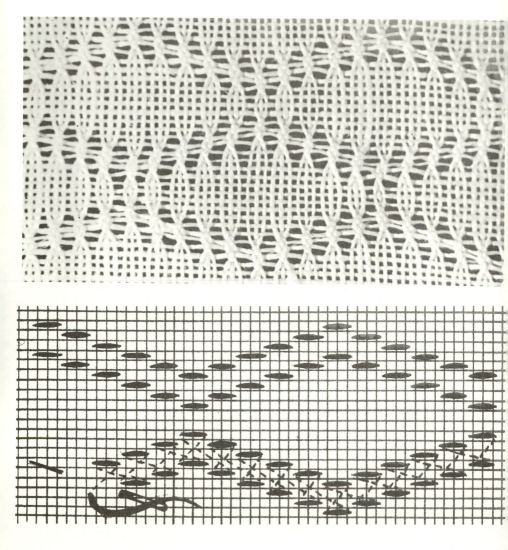

Triangle stitch is double back stitch sewn in a triangle, beginning as shown in the diagram. The stitch is worked in diagonal rows (***).

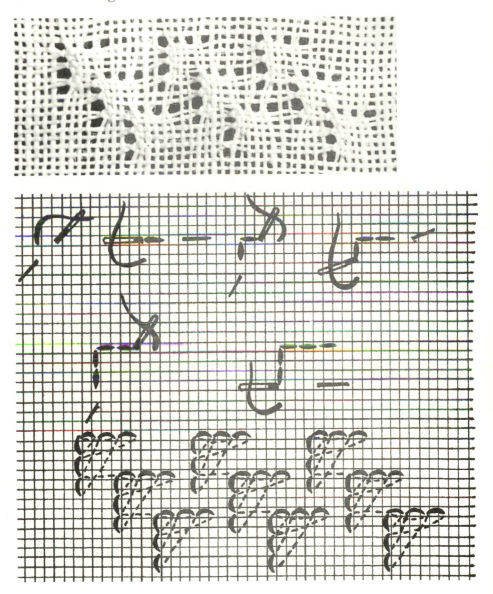

Square stitch can be worked in two ways: either work as
for triangle stitch but continue the stitch to complete
a square, which pulls the shape into a parallelogram,
or work double back stitch round the shape, beginning
at opposing corners and continuing in a clockwise
direction, which pulls neat squares as in the
photograph (***).

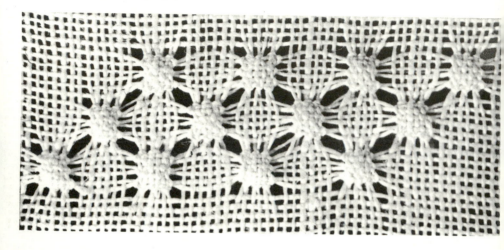

Braid stitch requires a large area to be seen at its best and should be worked on a frame, because the threads become distorted and confused otherwise (***).

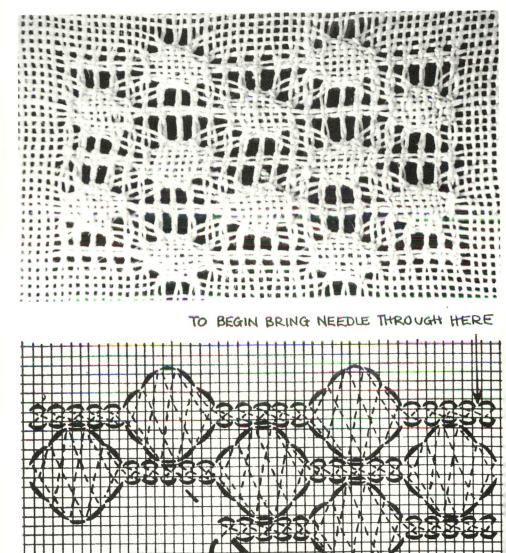

TO BEGIN BRING NEEDLE THROUGH HERE

FILLINGS BASED ON GREEK CROSS STITCH

The following five fillings are all Greek cross stitch, the only difference being the spacing of the crosses. Below is a diagram of Greek cross stitch and all the fillings are worked in diagonal rows of this stitch.

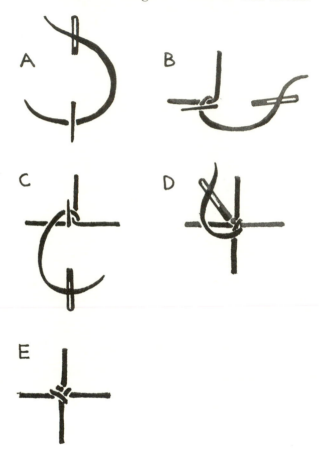

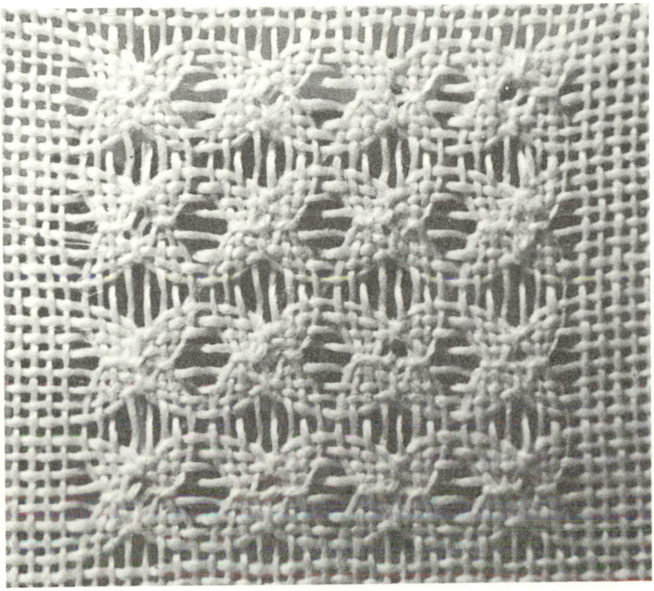

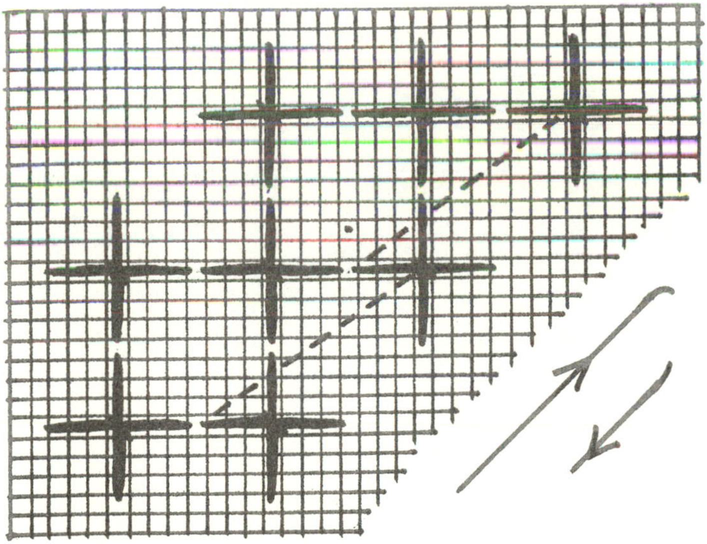

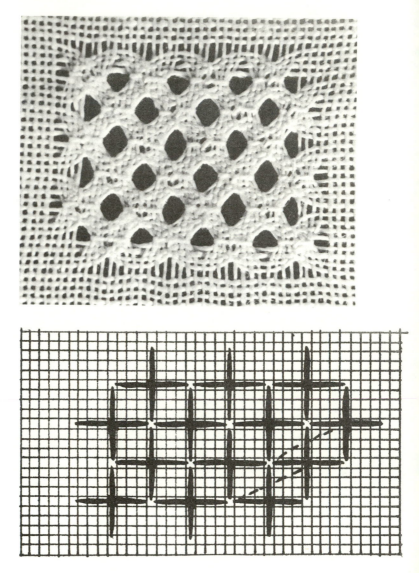

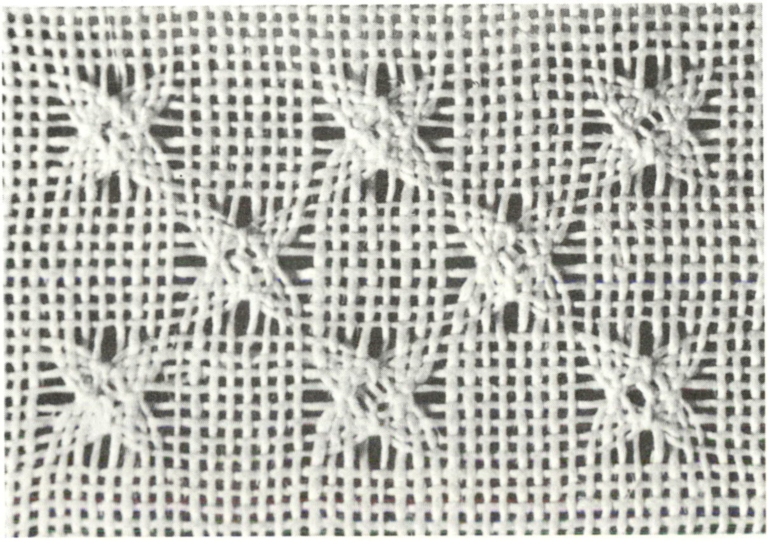

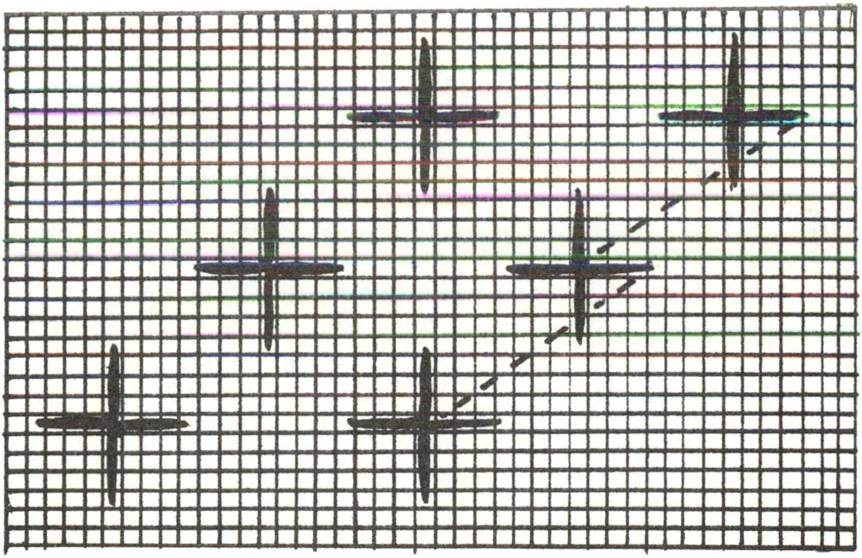

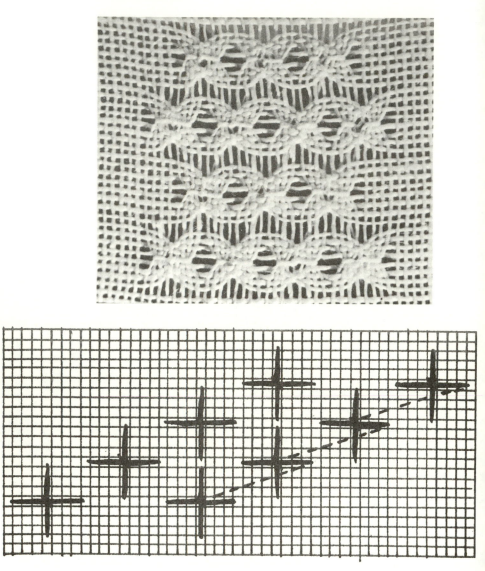

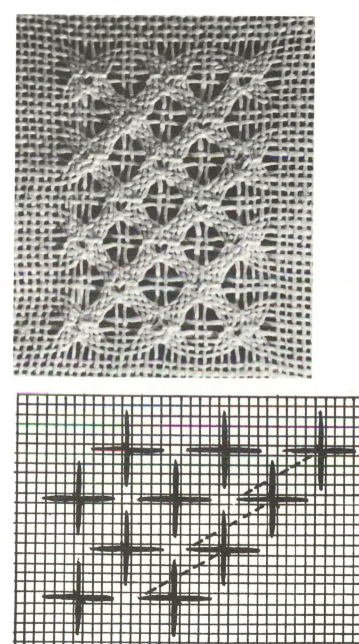

MISCELLANEOUS STITCHES

Indian drawn ground is worked in diagonal rows and the shape of the stitch is seen best on a fine openly woven material (***).

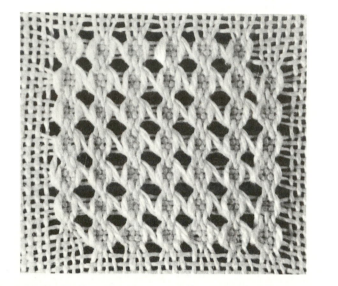

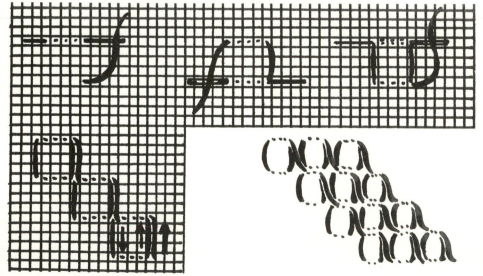

Drawn buttonhole is a form of buttonhole stitch worked on the counted thread. Two rows are worked back to back diagonally to form a ridge. Looks best in a twisted thick thread.

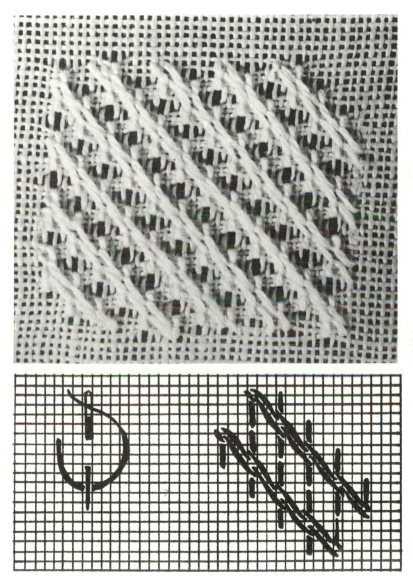

Rosette stitch

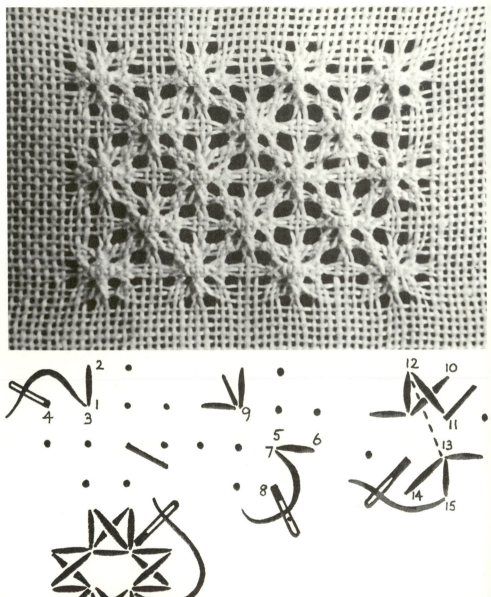

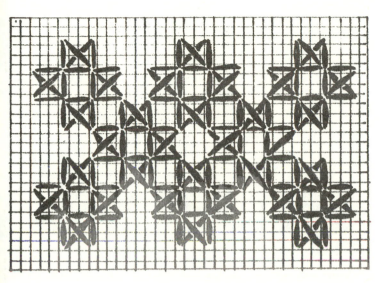

This is one of the most complicated stitches to learn, especially from a diagram, and although it looks effective when worked, chequer stitch has a similar appearance and is less complicated. The numbers on the diagram indicate order of working.

Four-sided stitch is a very versatile pulled stitch. Reading from A, the three movements are shown which build up each 'box' that forms the stitch. Note that the needle goes from corner to corner diagonally, making a cross stitch on the wrong side. B shows a method of turning a corner (***).

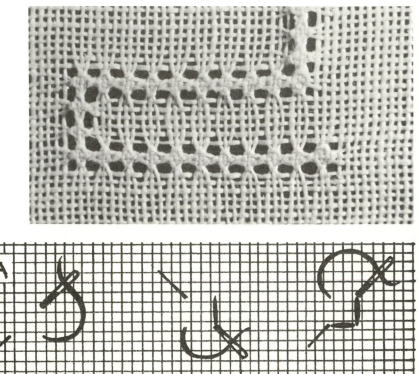

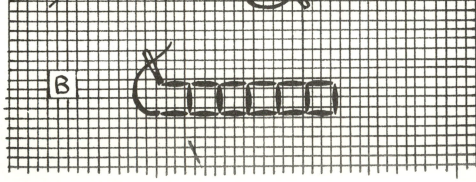

Three-sided stitch is a tricky stitch to master, but is well worth learning because it can be both a line stitch or a filling. Follow the movements shown in the diagram and when completed each stitch is double on the right side but diagonal stitches are single on the wrong side (***).

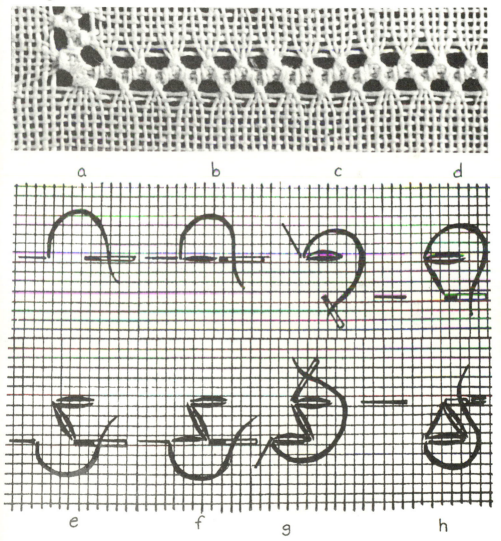

Eyelet stitch filling is a three-sided stitch worked in a circle from the same centre point to form an eyelet. Work in diagonal rows to make a filling.

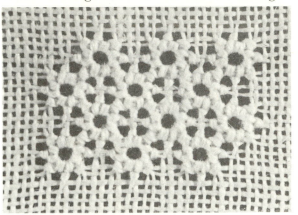

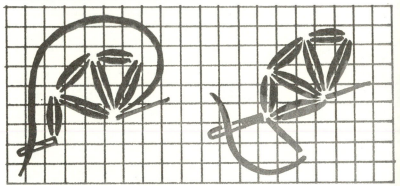

COMPOSITE STITCHES

Satin stitch and eyelet filling is exactly what its name suggests and can be followed from the diagram or illustration.

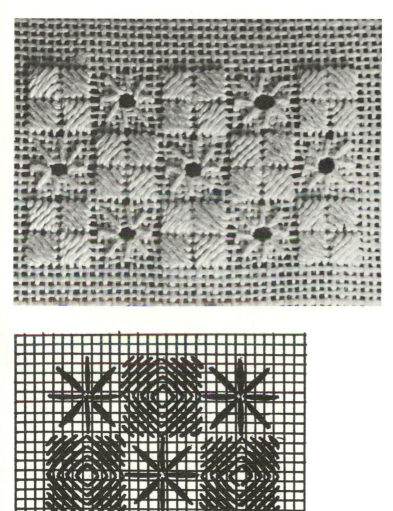

Diamond and spot filling

The diamonds are worked in either four-sided or single faggot stitch, with small satin stitch blocks in each.

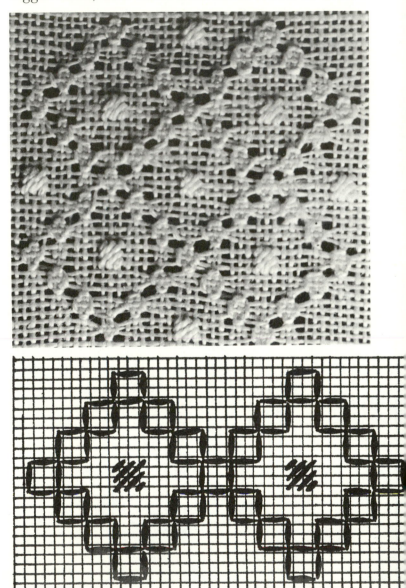

Greek cross and satin stitch filling

Satin stitch blocks are added to enrich a Greek cross filling.

Four-sided stitch and satin stitch filling

A single four-sided stitch and 4 satin stitches are worked alternately to form a row, which is repeated in brick formation to make a filling.

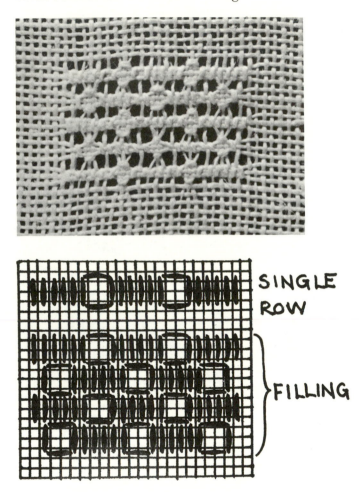

SINGLE ROW

FILLING

Eyelet and step stitch filling

A step stitch of 6 stitches over 3 threads is worked, and the spaces filled with a square eyelet over 8 threads, giving a bold, rich texture.

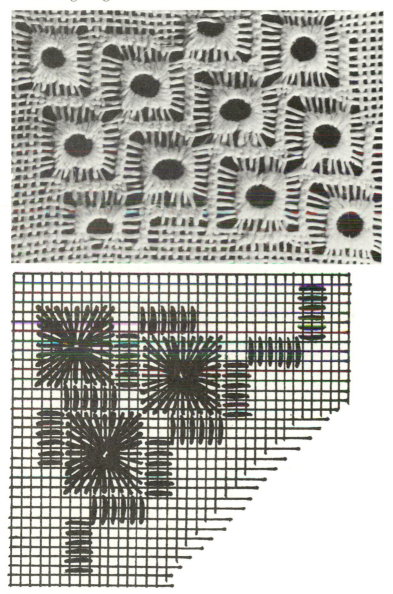

Outlined diamond filling

Diamond-shaped eyelets over 10 threads are separated by a diagonally worked satin stitch over 2 threads.

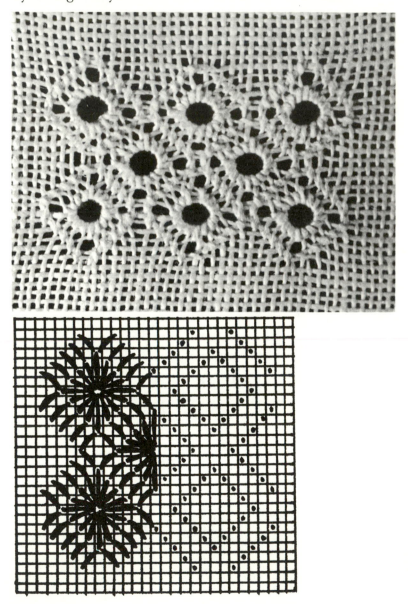

Thicket filling

Close rows of small square eyelets are worked over 4 threads alternating with 5 satin stitches over 2 threads (***).

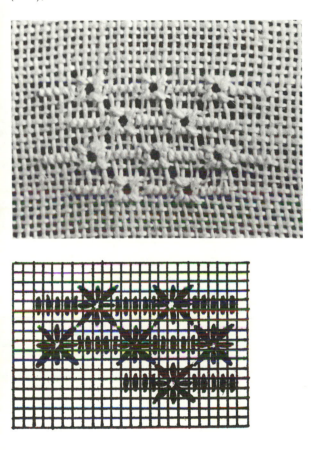

Reeded stitch

Close rows of 3 double back stitches over 5 threads, alternating with 5 satin stitches over 3 threads.

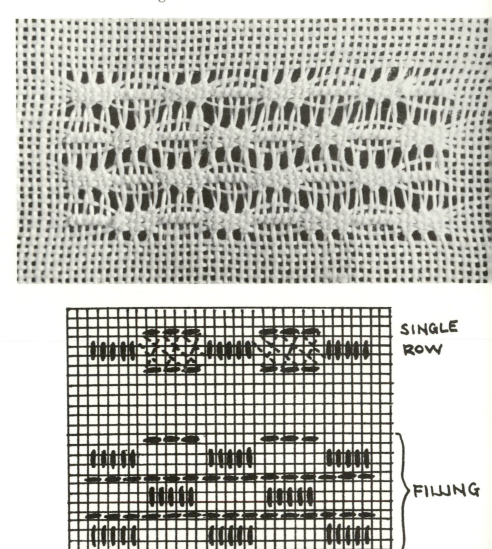

SINGLE ROW

FILLING

102

Mosaic filling

This is basically a square, bounded on each side by blocks of 5 satin stitches over 4 threads, in the centre of which a four-sided stitch is worked topped by a cross stitch. As well as forming a filling the squares may be used individually.

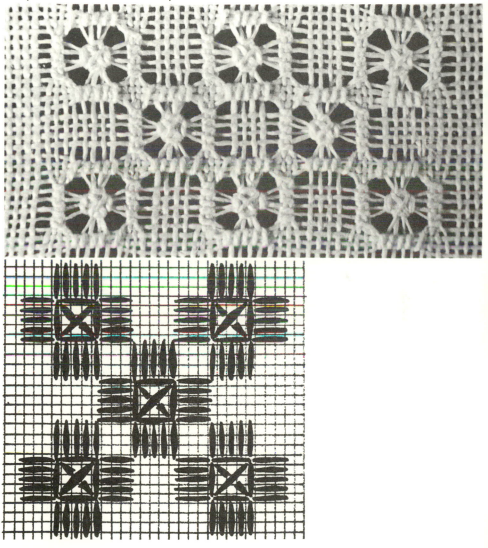

DESIGNING

To design for any method of embroidery it is necessary
to understand the basic technique in order that its
limitations are apparent. Pulled work is based largely
on horizontal and vertical rows, so that if these lines
can form the basis of a design the stitches will easily
take their part in it. There is no one way of designing
successfully, because it will depend to a great extent on
the individual's personality and talent, but like any skill
it has to be learnt and kept in practice. We do not
expect to appear on the centre court at Wimbledon
with only one tennis stroke, and yet many people are
discouraged because they do not achieve a
professional-looking design in one lesson.

Once a few basic stitches have been learnt, a limited
design can be built directly on to the material, either
as a border which could be applied in many practical
ways, or 'freely' to form an experimental shape for
either decorative or practical purposes.

The aim of the following pages is to show a beginner
how to start, and to suggest some ways of designing
so that by experiment it will be possible to develop
confidence and an ability to see potential ideas in the
shapes all around us in everyday life, for even a line
of socks reflected as a shape in double glazing can be
the basis of an apparently abstract design.

105

This satin-stitch motif could be used as a unit of design which could be repeated to form decoration on the mat below or continued as a border on bold hessian to form the decoration for a cushion.

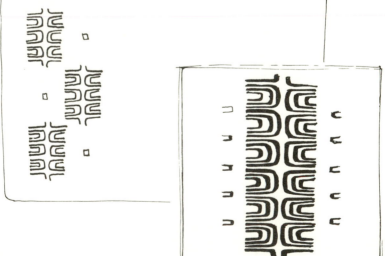

A simple border based on blocks of satin stitch, which can be counted from the photograph. This could be used on a bag of bold furnishing fabric or on a finer material for a household article such as a tea cosy.

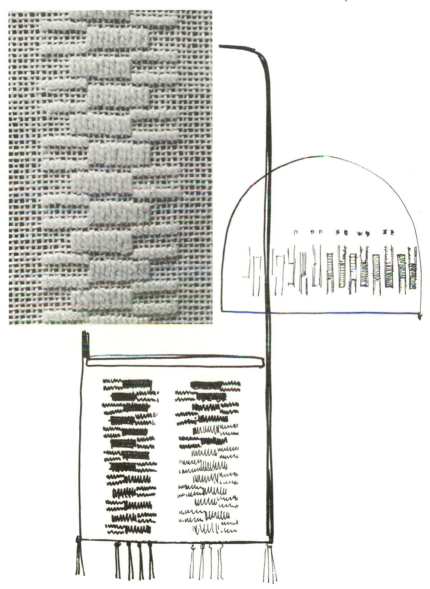

A border or unit of design based on satin stitch and diamond eyelets which could be worked finely for a collar and matching cuffs or on a coarser material to form the decoration round a box.

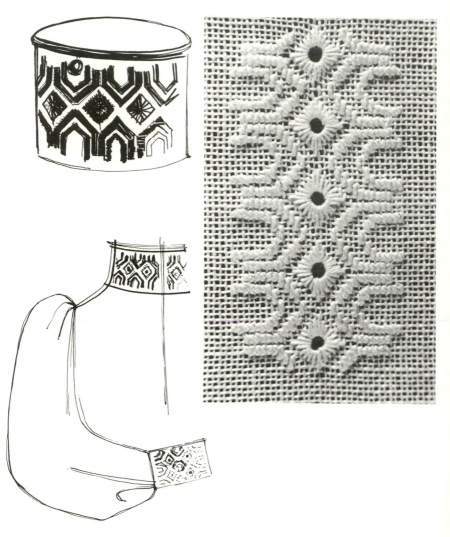

Three-sided stitch and satin stitch combine to form a border which has a feeling of movement. Worked very finely it could make an elegant pattern on a tie, or more boldly used, add richness to a pochette bag.

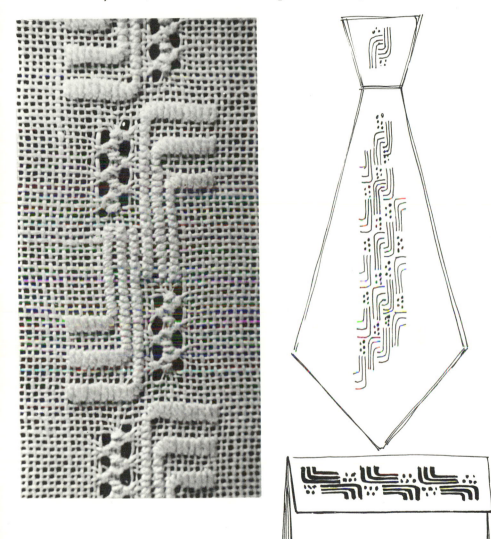

A narrow border in satin-stitch blocks and round eyelets could be repeated on the rectangular shape of mat or cushion, or used singly on a hair tie or band.

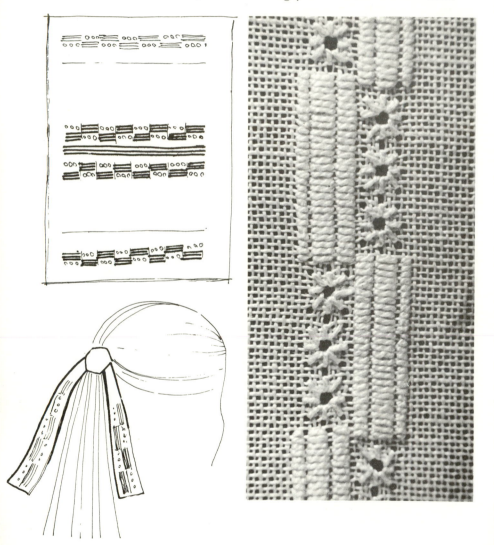

This border looks best on fine open material and could
be applied as a band round a lampshade or on
heavier material used to decorate a book mark.

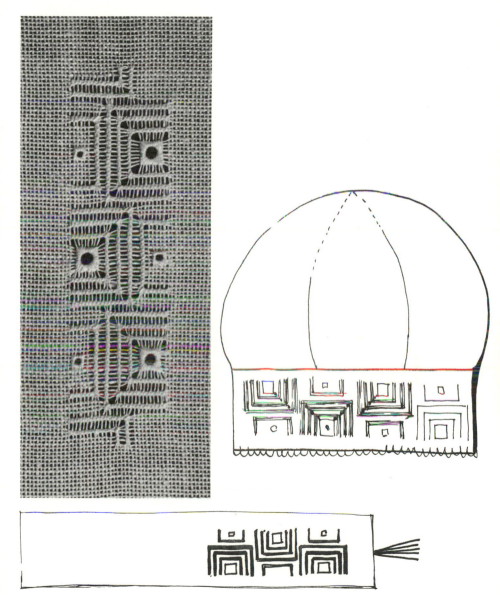

Three borders in satin stitch, combined with square eyelets, honeycomb stitch and oblong eyelets.

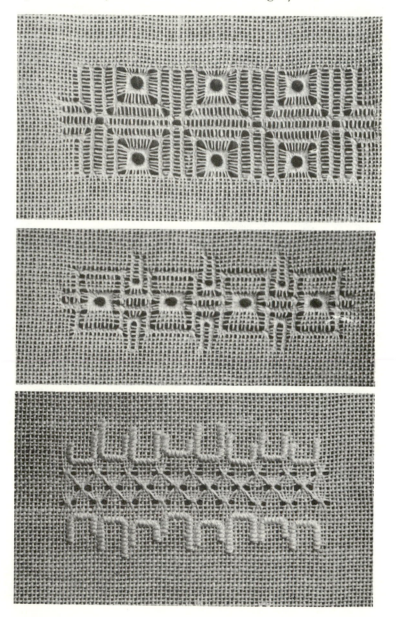

Corners of two conventionally worked napkins which
are part of a set of four. By working each differently
the working is made less tedious. Planned and
worked by Mrs. Wakeling. Stitches used: eyelets,
festoon, satin stitch and framed cross filling.

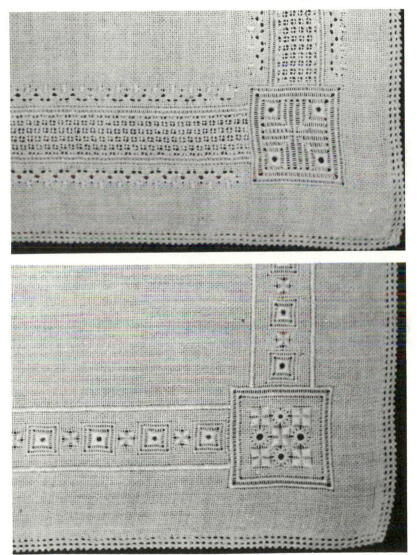

Two sides of the same lampshade in a red/pink/orange widely striped furnishing sheer; the pulled work was sewn directly on to the material after ascertaining exactly how much of the lampshade was seen at any one time. Stitches include eyelets, braid, Finnish and running.

115

Almost identical designs worked directly on to the material, illustrating the free use of pulled work. The mat is worked on white linen and the enlargement of the centre of another mat on scrim, incorporating satin stitch, eyelets and four-sided stitch. Designed and worked by Mrs. Edna Wark.

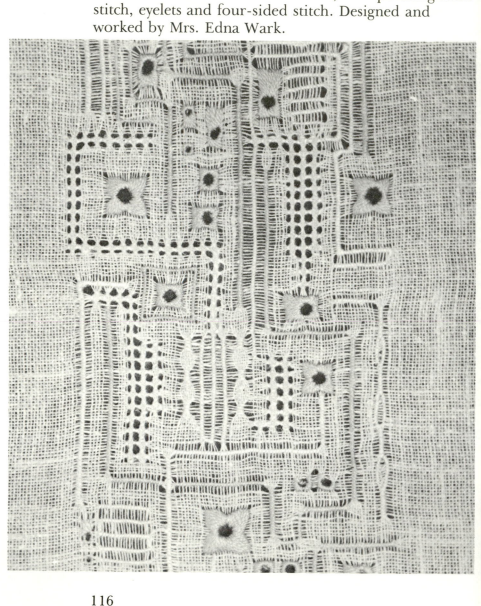

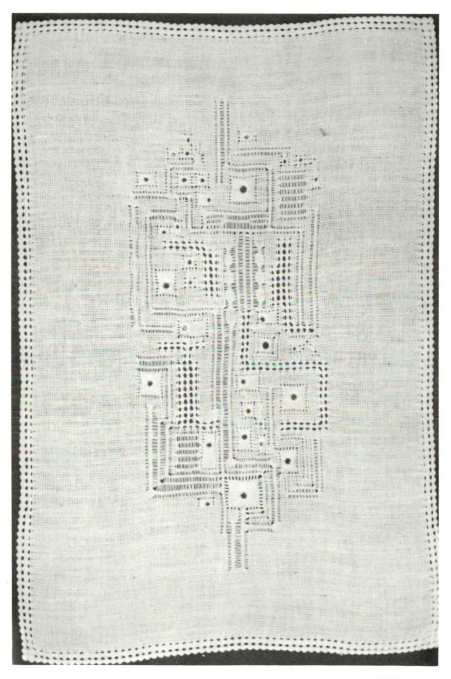

This flower is made up of three blocks of pulled fillings over which have been superimposed a free outline of Twilley's Bubbly knitting yarn which has added life and a feeling of movement. Twelve of these motifs, all slightly different, form the decoration on an attractive tablecloth, part of which is illustrated in the other photograph. Designed and worked by Mrs. Edna Wark.

The two trees on this page were built up directly on to the material in satin stitch, the detail being added when the trees were complete.

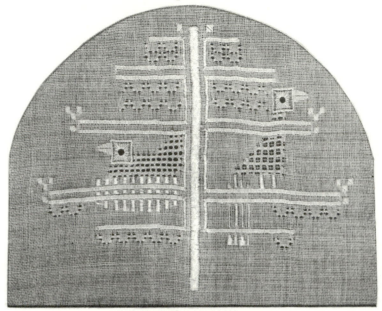

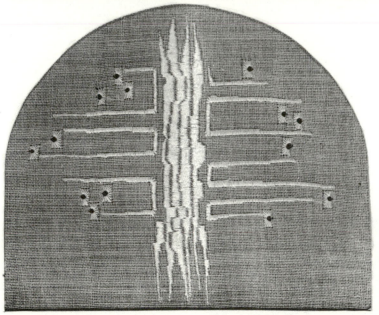

Part of a mat on pale green linen with simple white embroidery using satin stitch, honeycomb stitch and four-sided stitch with a picot edge, which because of its simplicity is very effective. Planned and worked by Mrs. Farrell.

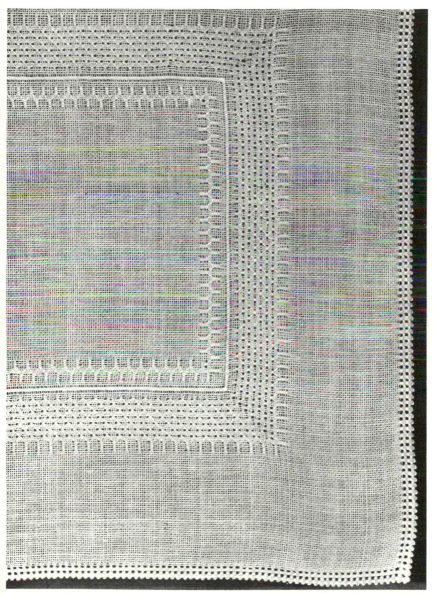

These examples, all worked directly on to the fabric, were based on the same exercise in which the students were limited to 2 stitches, satin stitch and eyelets, and two thicknesses of thread. The schoolgirls are in their second year of embroidery only.

Helga Clarke worked this example, which resembles a stylised tree.

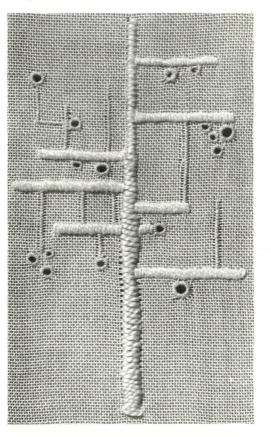

Opposite:
Hazel Crellin shows an unusual approach in working her example in black but mounting it on glittery paper to give it life.

122

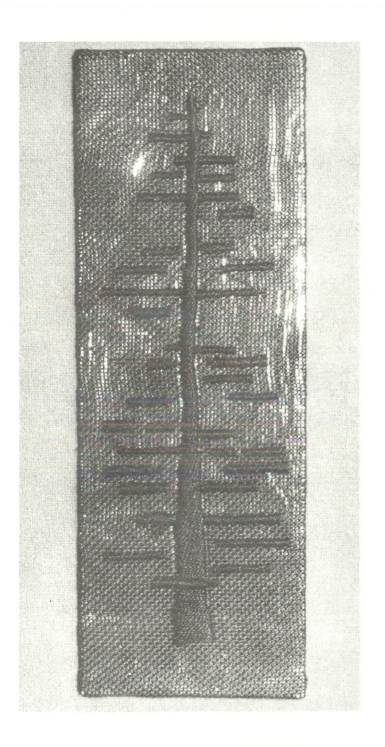

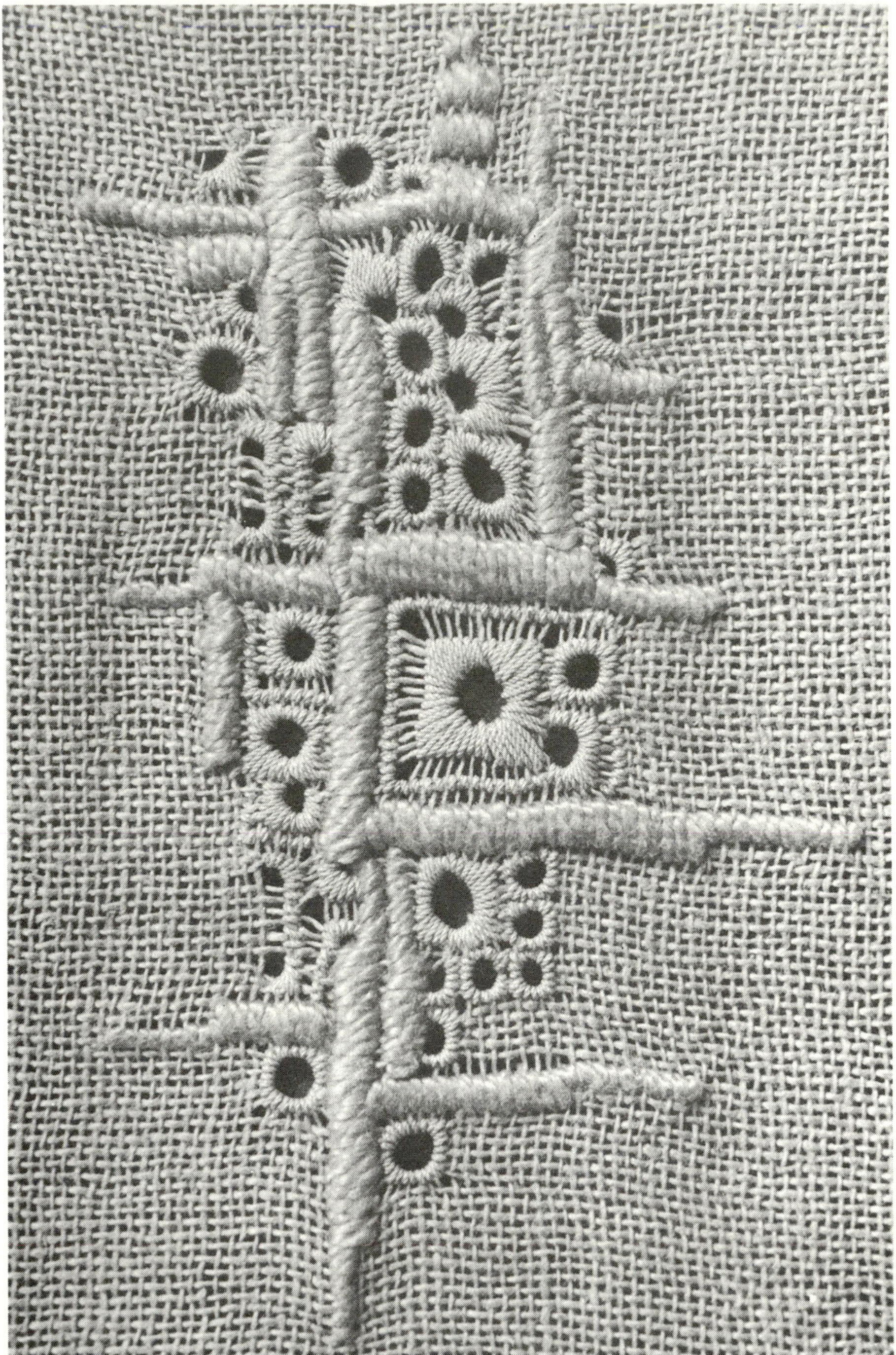

Opposite:
Mrs. Strafford is an experienced needlewoman and in her exercise has produced an attractive modern motif yet still retaining the competence of traditional techniques.

A sampler of free pulled shapes incorporating some needleweaving, by Alison Barrell.

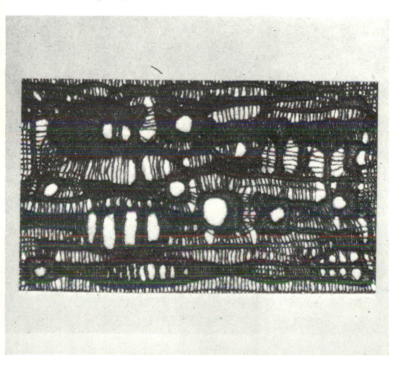

Overleaf:
The letter P worked in lines of four-sided stitch and both tensioned and loosely worked satin stitch. The upright lines are of unequal length to avoid giving too sharp and formal a shape to the letter.

125

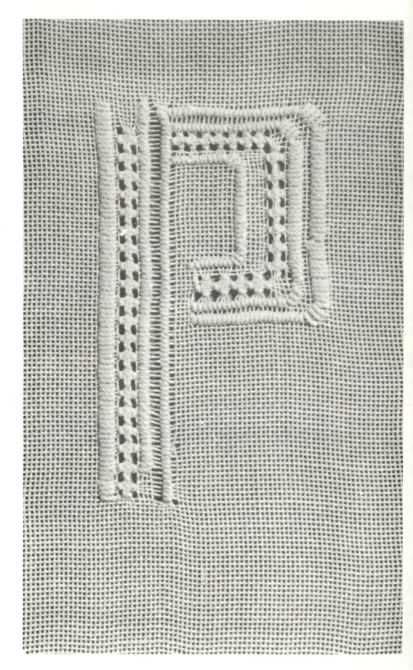

Most people, however lacking in confidence, are able to construct a grid, which can be tacked or worked directly on to the material in outline. The grid may be even or asymmetrical (below) or a loose construction of lines (below right) and may be interpreted in a variety of ways. The lines could be satin stitch, back stitch, four-sided or three-sided stitch, in fact any line stitch, though probably a smooth stitch would be the best foil for pulled fillings which can be used to texture some of the areas formed by the grid. The grid can be the basis of both practical and decorative items. from a pincushion to a large hanging.

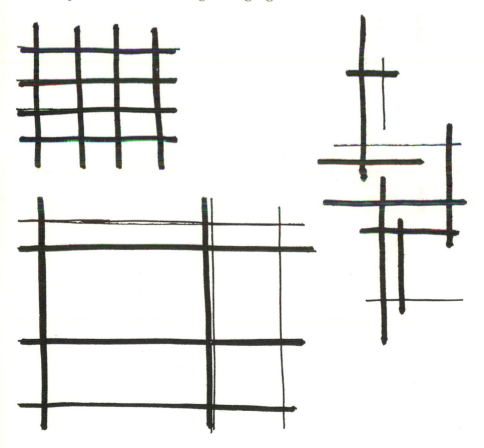

prices are,
mining th
ments, an
are likely
important
Where
ments? In
pay large
agricultur
should ov
output in
tion in th
may also
foodstuffs
advantage
probably
food consu
that the n
could be a
this Britai
imports a
On the
Britain a
expand m
effect of F

the first p
annual in
al fund.
r the years
Britain, wh
e volume
be increa
where Brit
s. Moreove
slow down
mption in F
et reductio
s much as
n would ha
mounting to
industrial
nd the C
ore rapidly.
igher prices

tent factor in deter-
demands and settle-
s angle, British costs
pidly than in other
countries.
the balance of pay-
Britain will have to
nts to the common
higher farm prices
lt in increased farm
vill lead to a reduc-
od imports. There
exports of certain
as some productive
her food prices will
rate of growth of
n. PROSPECT believes
the food import bill
million, but against
o pay levies on these
ut £200 million.
unt, trade between
on Market would
bearing in mind the
l the spur which this

pr
end
be s
to t
and
arra
move
1973,
ment
paym
the ad
In this
be felt
The
pound
ment.
provided
allow Br
Special
recent IM
payments
tion, PROS
will deri
transition

bably rise to about
l of the transition per
These strands in the ba
ummarized as follows.
he UK will be some
£500 million per ann
gements will be su
ment will build up
for example, the fir
may produce an
nts effect of about
verse effect may be
progression the m
in 1978.
interesting quest
ould stand the st
The difficulties
l that the Comm
itain to make fr
Drawing Rights
IF arrangements
to the Commi
PECT believes th
ve important
period. ∎

The exploded shape is now well known as the basis for design, the system being to cut into pieces of assorted sizes any simple basic shape and move them apart.

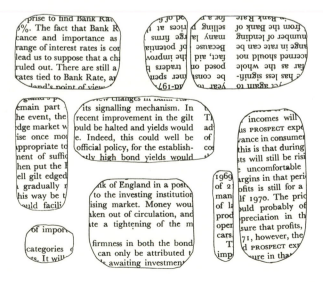

Attention should be paid to the background shapes that emerge and not only the shape of each section of cut paper. On the left are two shapes exploded from a square, the top one having been cut vertically and the other one both horizontally and vertically, after which the shapes were rounded. This suggested an interesting background shape, and the photograph shows an interpretation of the design by working single faggot stitch on a curtain fabric in different sizes in the background area.

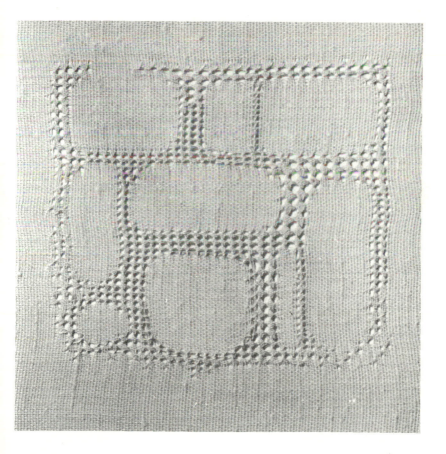

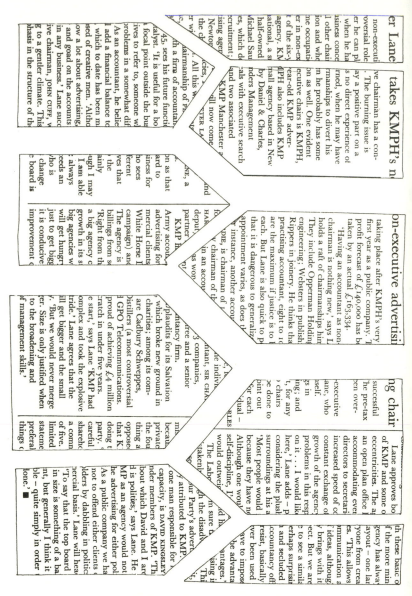

Another version of the exploded shape based on an oblong. The design has been purposely made slightly irregular to avoid exact repetition, which would be boring to work and look at. The interpretation in embroidery shows a subtle use of pulled work; stitches

130

used are festoon, ringed back, Greek cross, reeded,
Finnish and satin stitch on a deep rose-red furnishing
fabric. Designed and worked by Miss Diana Dalmahoy.

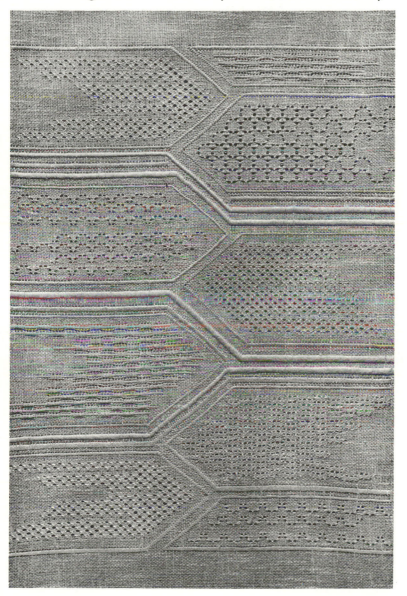

A circle is the basis of this exploded design seen in cut paper and embroidery; as well as pulled thread techniques an area of encroaching Gobelin has been worked as a contrast in texture. Free couched outlines have been superimposed on the design to link the basic shapes; the ground is emerald green Moygashel and on it are worked matching threads of Anchor Soft, *coton à broder* and stranded cotton.

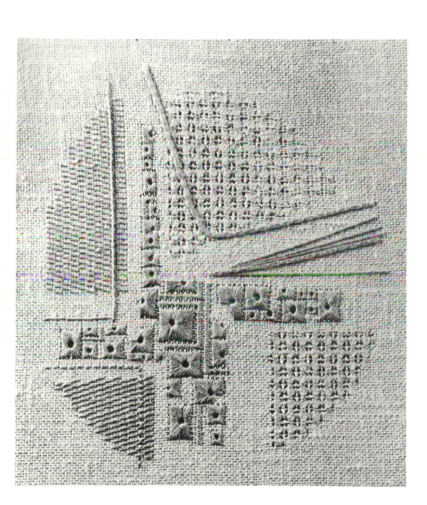

Natural forms may also be exploded; in these
examples paper shapes were cut from actual leaves and
segmented to make further shapes. It is interesting
that many exploded leaves suggest flower shapes.

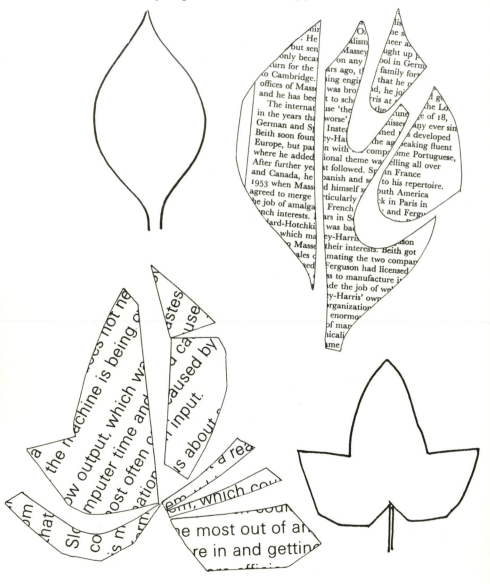

This design was based on actual leaf shapes which have become formalised by their simple decorative treatment. Stitches used on a dark brown linen are ringed back, ripple, tensioned satin and buttonhole, wave, double back and encroaching Gobelin. Designed and worked by Mrs. Jennifer Frost.

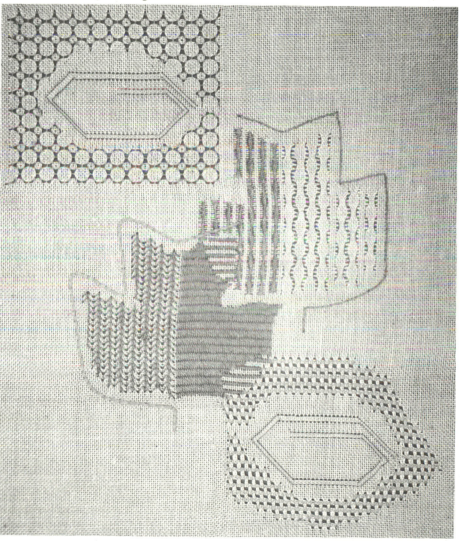

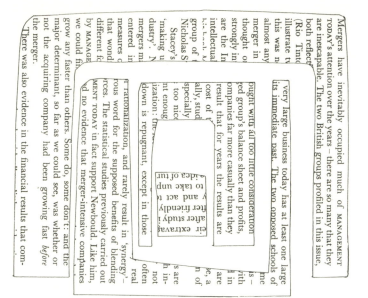

These are not true exploded shapes but are all cut from a basic square from which some pieces have been removed. They could be used to decorate a book cover, enlarged for a cushion, mat or panel, or increased further in scale for a hanging.

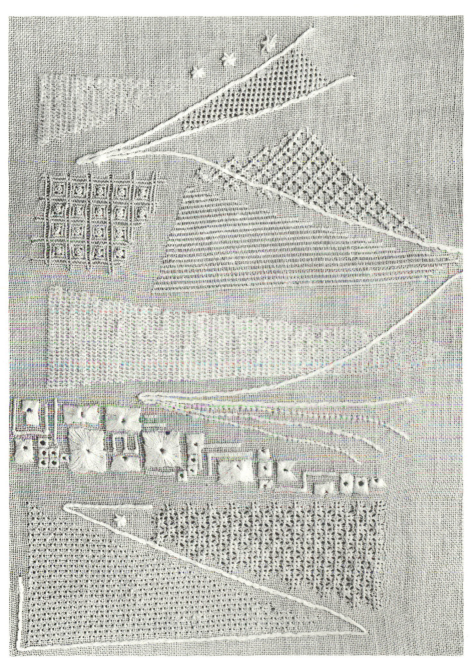

Previous page:
A tray cloth based on cut paper shapes by a worker
who had not previously attempted modern pulled
thread but had a sound basic technique. Designed and
worked on white linen by Mrs. Akers.

Linear doodles based on horizontal and vertical lines
are another suggestion for beginning a design and
ideas can be derived from town planning maps, wiring
circuits or technical drawings. Despite being linear they
enclose geometric areas particularly suited to pulled
thread fillings. Such a design can be planned directly
on to material by pinning thread or string to shape on
the fabric, and then the basic outlines can be made
both subtle and interesting by thoughtful use of varied
stitchery as is suggested by the different thicknesses of
line in the illustrations.

As lettering is essentially a linear craft it is particularly difficult to translate into acceptable terms for pulled thread, but it is not impossible. If lettering is to be read it must be clearly legible, but letters may also be combined to form a unit of design for use on personal objects; box top, belt or tie, for example.

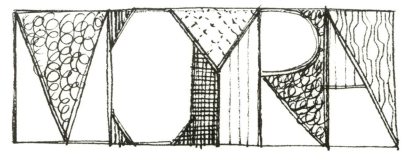

On this page are shown three ideas for lettering in pulled work based on short names, and initials could be similarly used. In 'Moyra' the background divisions form the letters, which need only thin outlining with pulled fillings worked between them. 'Pam' is entirely linear so would be worked in close rows of line stitches such as satin, back and double back, three- and four-sided. A closely worked stitch, such as double faggot, would form the background of 'Gay', leaving only a minimal outline to be sewn.

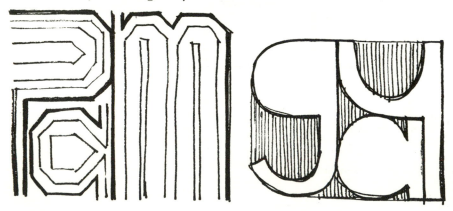

The design of the mat is based on the name 'Brian' and is worked on white linen in satin stitch (used vertically and horizontally) in thick thread contrasted with bold areas of fillings. The hem is wide in order to frame the design.

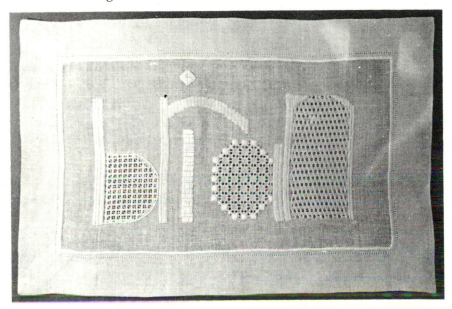

A quotation could form the basis of a design for church embroidery, which the sketch illustrates, the angular shapes being dictated by the method.

Natural forms such as birds, fish and plants can be reduced decoratively into very simple shapes and yet still be recognisable. On these pages are designs of birds made up of vertical, horizontal and diagonal lines enclosing geometric areas that will readily translate into pulled thread. Other subject matter already based on geometric forms are buildings, from stately homes and churches to small houses, ships of all ages, and machinery.

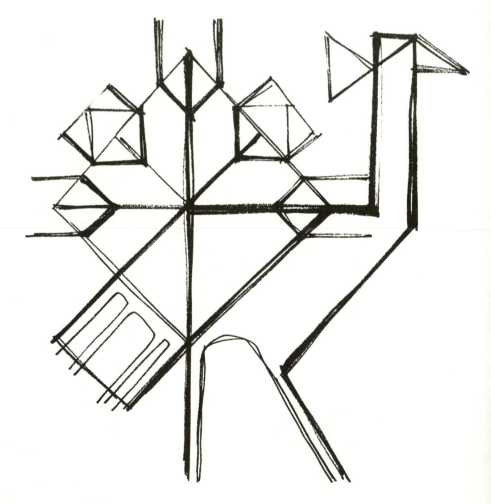

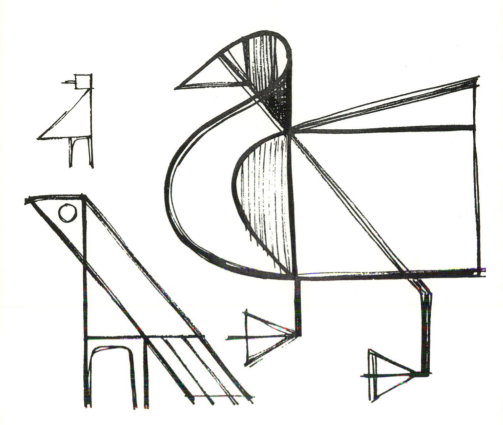

Overleaf left:
'Drumnadrochit'; a panel of a fish in a combination of techniques including appliqué, surface stitchery, pulled thread, with some mica and shisha glass. The whole panel is in rich colours of wine red on a deep blue striped furnishing fabric using a wide selection of threads. Designed and worked by Mrs. Ryrie.

Overleaf right:
A very stylised peacock forms the basic design of this sampler which was among the prizewinners in an international sampler competition in 1967. Both cream *coton à broder* and olive green stranded cotton are used on an off-white linen to show a variety of fillings. Designed and worked by Mrs. Monica Spanton.

143

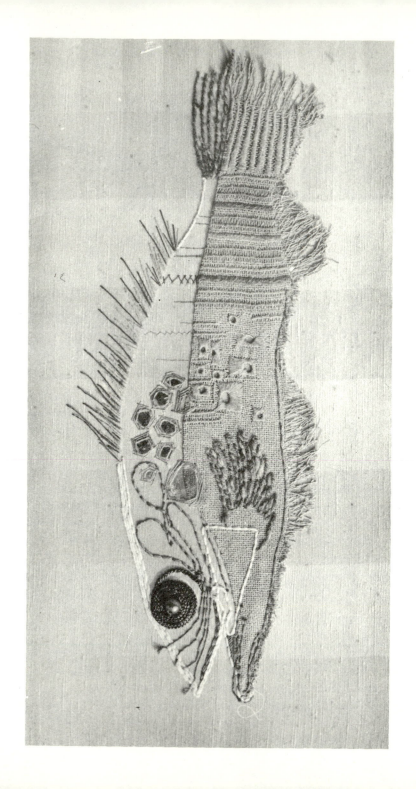

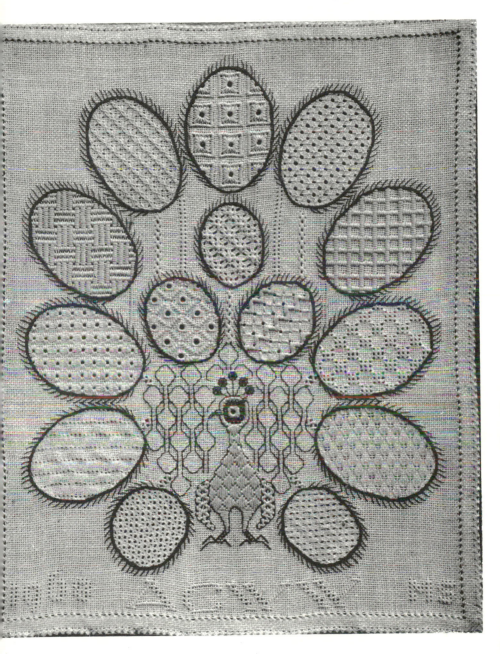

Two sections of a panel by M. Cole incorporating an inventive combination of pulled and drawn thread work and padded appliqué on white in shades of blue.

Opposite:
Panel in builder's scrim illustrating a vigorous use of free pulled thread in combination with other techniques. Designer/executant Alison Barrell.

146

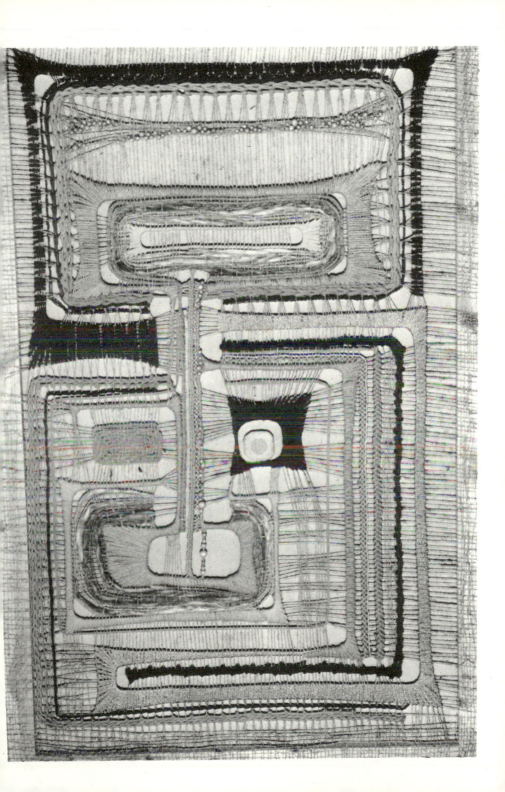

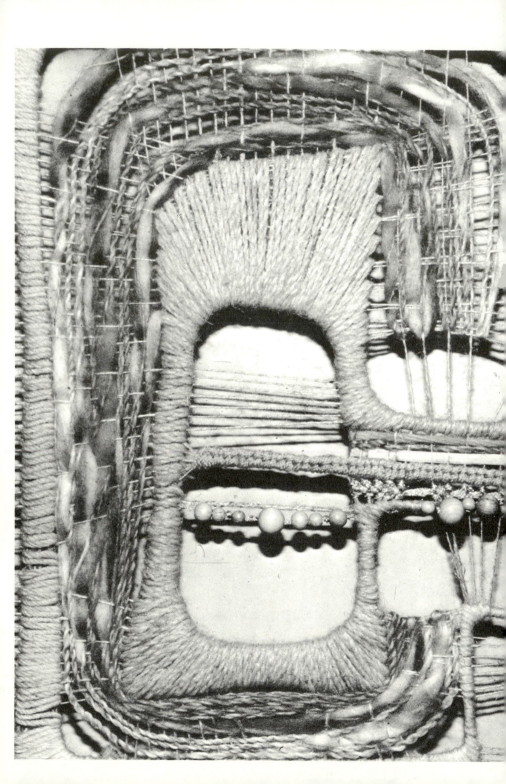

Opposite:
An enlargement of part of the previous panel clearly illustrating the use of surface stitchery, darning and beads in conjunction with a magnificently bold eyelet hole.

Below:
Thickly grouped dark red warp threads are stretched in front of a richly coloured and textured ground, and although this panel is not true pulled thread it does suggest a direction for further experiment. Designer/ executant Marjorie Self.

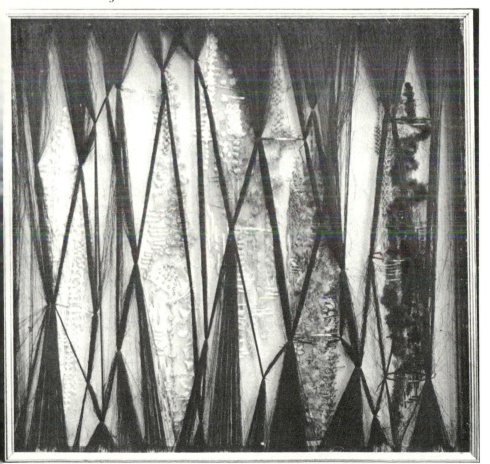

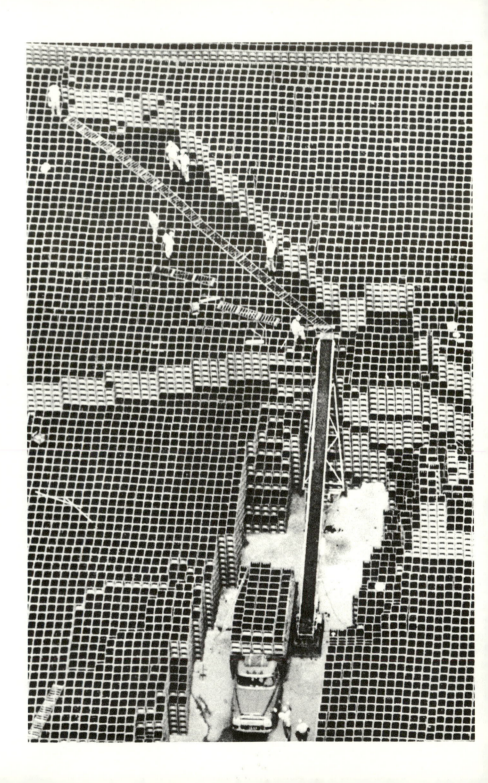

Opposite:
This photograph from Japan of beer crates in a yard
was taken from a helicopter at such an arresting angle
that it has become an abstract design; because of the
geometric shapes, translation into a counted thread
method is immediately suggested. In many similar
ways, actual objects can be the root of 'abstract'
designs. (By courtesy of the Press Association.)
Below:
'Rock Pool' is an imaginative amalgam of techniques in
a three-dimensional panel. The top surface is window-
cleaner's scrim with cut and pulled eyelets, shapes
padded and satin-stitched or whipped, surrounding a
large hole through which is seen an area of texture
underneath. Designer/executant Pat Wood.

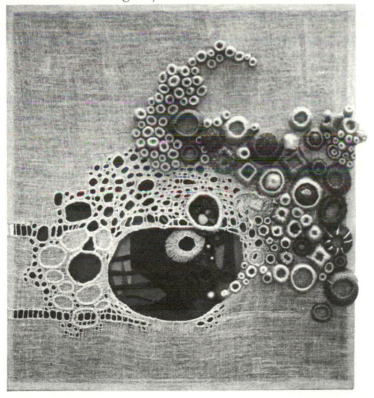

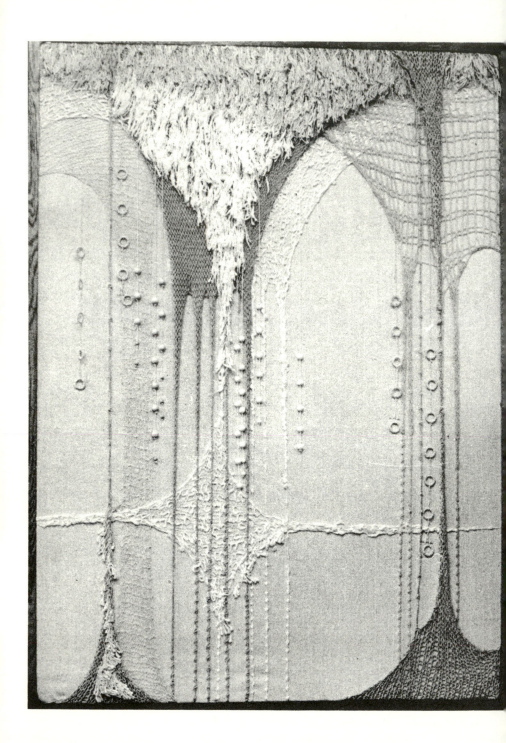

Opposite:
This panel illustrates a new idea of pulling. A fabric is formed, in this instance by knitting, and is pulled to shape and attached to a background. The shapes here suggest architectural forms and have been enriched with beads, fringed Twilley's Bubbly and covered rings. The panel is in muted colours of pink, brown and off-white. Designer/executant Margaret Gabay.

Overleaf left:
Part of a hanging in builder's scrim demonstrating that movement and life can be achieved in pulled thread by bold designing. Free pulled thread is worked with wool, string, flax and unwoven ground threads, together with some fringing and plaiting which combine to make a most satisfying and lively hanging. Designer/executant Barbara Siedlecka.

Overleaf right:
A richly coloured and textured panel incorporating a variety of techniques, including pulled thread, in a 'layer' design suggesting rock formation. Designer/executant Alison Barrell.

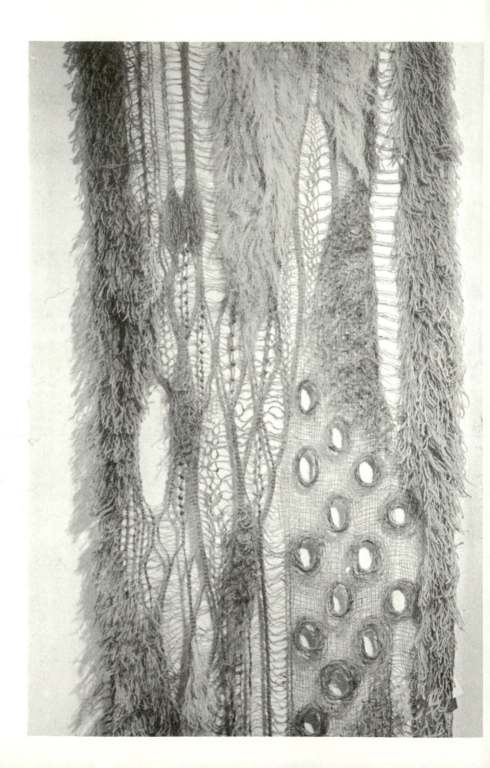

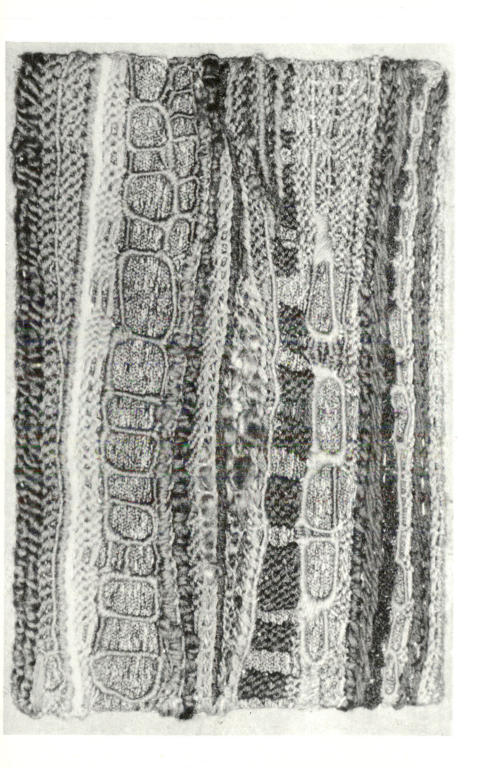

EDGINGS

Because pulled work is particularly suitable for utilitarian articles of dress and household linen, many edgings have been evolved based on pulled thread stitches, but they should always be considered as an integral part of the overall design of an article. An eye-catching edging can detract from the rest of the embroidery or even cause a confused and muddled effect because the article has been over-elaborated. If the edging is rich and interesting this might prove sufficient decoration for some items, leaving the rest of the article completely plain to show it to best effect.

If it is intended to combine an edging with other embroidery the edging should be considered and worked last, when it will be more obvious what is required; simply leave plenty of material to allow for its formation. There can be no set rules for width of hem as this will depend on many factors – purpose, weight of fabric, boldness or otherwise of the rest of the design – and the choice rests on individual judgment and selection.

Corners can be a problem, and it is well worth learning to mitre a corner well, although in Scandinavian work corners are not often mitred and yet they look neat.

In the following pages are just a few permutations on the theme of pulled thread edgings, concentrating on

157

the actual finishing of the edge rather than rich decoration which could be formed by adding borders to edgings.

HOW TO MITRE A CORNER

A mitred corner is stitched on the cross and the most important point is to handle the material as lightly as possible to avoid stretching.

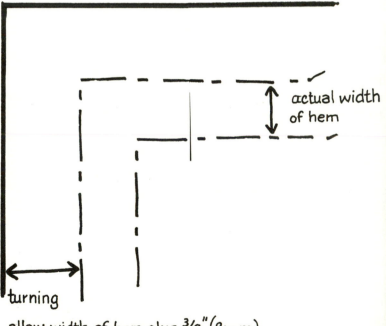

actual width of hem

turning

allow width of hem plus ³⁄₈″ (8mm)

Mark final hem lines in tacking to begin, exactly on the thread of the material.

158

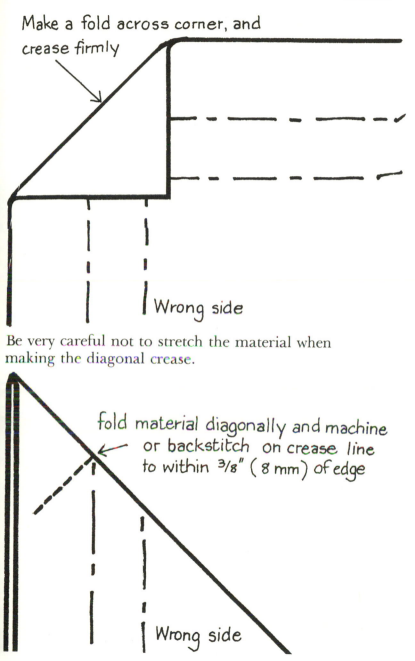

Make a fold across corner, and crease firmly

Wrong side

Be very careful not to stretch the material when making the diagonal crease.

fold material diagonally and machine or backstitch on crease line to within 3/8" (8 mm) of edge

Wrong side

Cut off excess material, press seam
open flat and snip off corners

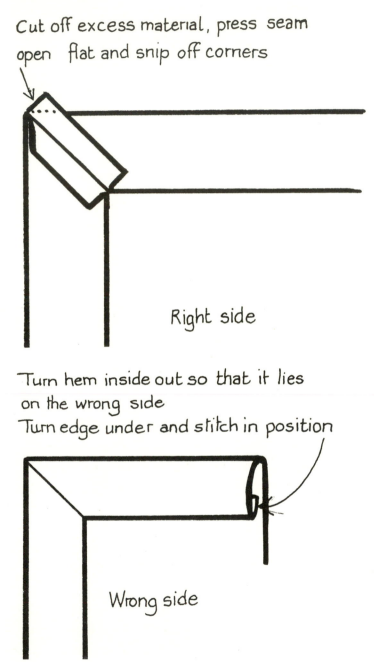

Right side

Turn hem inside out so that it lies
on the wrong side
Turn edge under and stitch in position

Wrong side

Simple faced edge: cut a piece of material for facing from fine linen or cotton exactly the same size and shape as the embroidered piece. Put article and facing right sides together and tack and machine on finished hem line, leaving about 3″ (8 cm) unstitched, in the middle of one side. Trim corners, turn through to right side and slip stitch opening together. After a light press the edge may be secured by a row of stitching about $\frac{3}{8}$″ (1 cm) from the edge. This method is particularly suitable for place mats as the facing forms an extra layer for heat resistance.

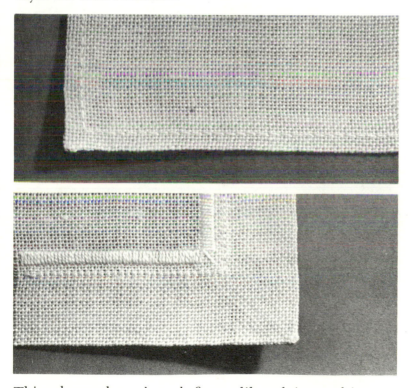

This edge makes a broad, frame-like edging and is wide in proportion to the whole article, whether mat or cloth. Leave $\frac{1}{2}$″ (1·5 cm) in addition to hem-turning allowance. Mitre corners but do not turn under edge.

Tack hem in position and work a broad counted satin stitch through both layers of fabric from the right side. To secure hem finally work a row of back stitch or double running stitch about 3 or 4 threads on the outer side of the satin stitch. Lastly trim off excess material on the wrong side close to the satin stitch.

Although much narrower, this hem is worked in a very similar way to the previous one, the hem being secured by two rows of satin stitch worked side by side and pulled fairly tightly; the excess material is trimmed off on the wrong side only when both rows of satin stitch are completed.

This hem is begun in the same way as the previous two, but when a row of satin stitch is completed, work a row of double wave stitch on the outer side of the satin stitch, trim off any excess material on the wrong side and work another row of double wave stitch on the inner edge.

Hem-stitched hem: mitre corners and tack hem in position exactly on the grain of the material. A thread may be withdrawn before beginning the hem stitch, though there is the opinion that this weakens the hem if the article is to be laundered frequently.

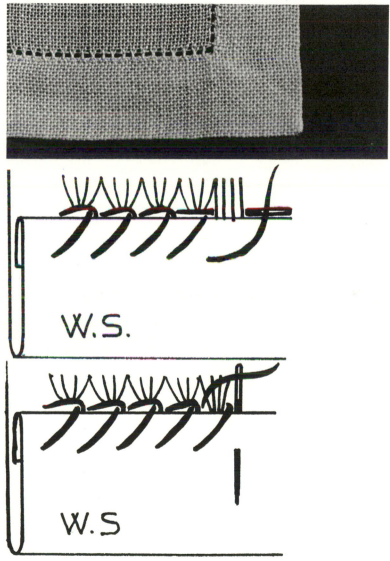

W.S.

W.S

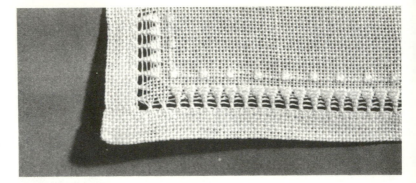

A hem-stitched hem with satin-stitch decoration. The hem stitch is worked over 4 threads and the satin stitch over the same groups of threads, with small satin-stitch spots over every other block. Tension variation makes the satin-stitch blocks into a triangular shape.

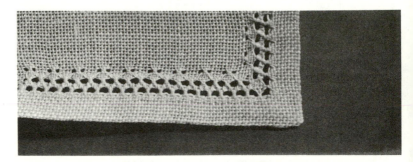

Another hem-stitched hem, after which three-sided stitch is worked over the same groups of threads and a row of honeycomb stitch next to the three-sided stitch.

PICOT EDGINGS

The following picot edgings are only three of many ways in which these edgings may be made. By removing a thread before working the first line of stitching in any of the methods a sharper picot will be formed.

Picot edge 1

Three satin stitches are worked over 4 threads tightly in a consecutive line, marking the finished edge of the article.

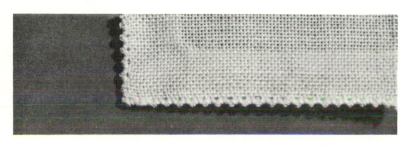

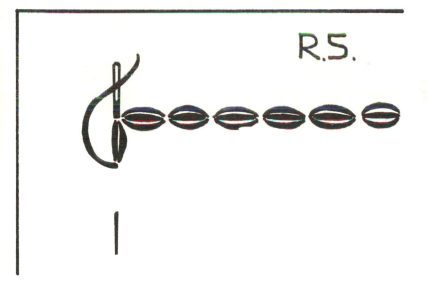

Fold material over so that the stitches are exactly on the edge of the fold and work thus:

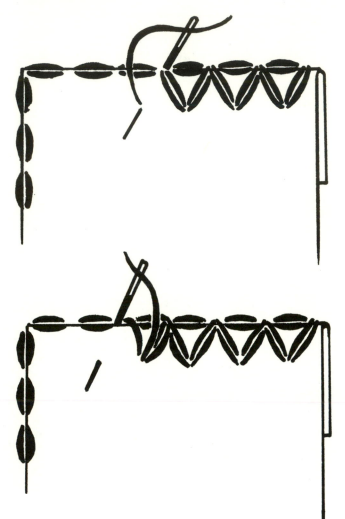

Finally turn hem under and hem lightly on the wrong side.

166

Picot edge 2

Work 4 buttonhole stitches over the same 4 threads, pulling tightly, and continue in this manner along a line marking the finished edge of the article.

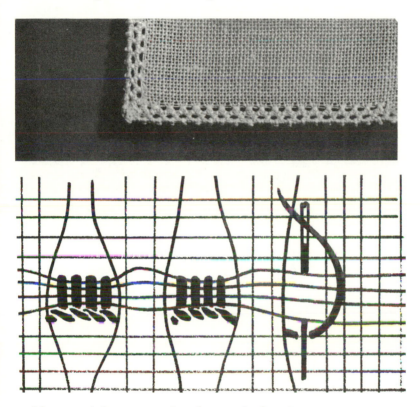

Fold material over so that buttonhole picots are on edge of fold and work three-sided stitch through both layers of material from the right side. Trim off raw edge close to three-sided stitch on the wrong side.

Picot edge 3

Begin by working hem stitch tightly on the wrong side
of the material over about 4 threads. Fold material
over so that the horizontal stitch lies on the edge of the
fold. Using the same holes as the hem stitching, work
the following stitch through both layers of material.

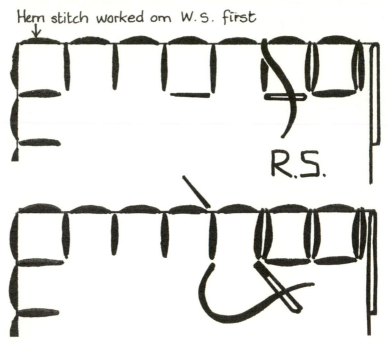

Hem stitch worked om W.S. first

R.S.

Trim off any surplus material on the wrong side close
to the stitching.

Decorated picot edge

Work picot edge 3, trim material and then work three close rows of four-sided stitch. Leave about 3 threads and work a line of satin stitch. Leave another 3 threads and work two rows of honeycomb stitch.

This edging is sufficiently rich to form the main decoration of an item such as a small cloth or mat.

FRINGED EDGING

Work two rows of three-sided stitch the required distance from the edge and fringe material away only when stitching is complete. This edging is not suitable for frequent laundering.

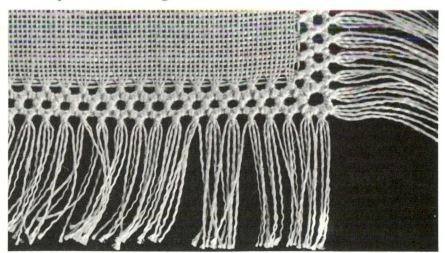

PULLED WORK IN THE PAST

In the comparatively short time available for preparation of a book of this sort it was only possible to see a limited selection of extant examples of pulled work, mainly in England, and therefore this chapter is not intended as a comprehensive survey of historical pulled work but rather as a guide to the reader to show how some embroiderers in the past have interpreted this method in ways which were influenced by their environment, the materials available to them, and contemporary fashions in clothes and furnishings.

In sketches, photographs and descriptions it is only possible to give an overall impression of any one piece, and it is far more valuable to go to a museum to see actual examples to truly appreciate the work of any one period, or even to assess why you dislike it. If the period sought is not on show, do not hesitate to ask if the museum has examples in its collections, as it may be possible to view pieces not on public display by arrangement with the museum authorities, who are usually extremely helpful.

Pulled work was often used on practical articles of dress and household linen. Many must have been lost in the inevitable process of wear and tear, laundering and decay, and sections or fragments of some pieces are now all that remain and it is only possible to guess at their original size and purpose. Purposes change too, and an article that was fairly commonplace two centuries ago may now extend our imaginations in trying to guess its original function; the success of television programmes where experts endeavour to place and date antiques confirms this difficulty in all fields of art and craft work. Textiles are also easily portable, so that their present resting place may be hundreds of miles away from their place of origin, and to fix a precise date and place of origin is work of detection and assumption. But looking at historical pieces of pulled work is extremely informative and at times quite stimulating when it is realised what a variety of ideas have been expressed in embroidery in the past; and as embroiderers of the second half of the twentieth century it is humbling to find that we do not have an exclusive claim to inventive and imaginative work, but that in the past our predecessors were equally willing to experiment with stitches, fabrics and a combination of techniques. It would appear that only in the early part of this century were strictures laid down on the 'correct' pulled thread technique, which led to much work of an extremely high technical standard but in many cases combined with stultified design: an approach that has not yet disappeared.

Unlike blackwork, pulled work does not have any distinctive style or period but tends to have a chameleon quality depending on which style of design and technique it is linked to, and the earliest pulled stitches may be just a few stitches worked more tightly than their fellows, as may be seen in odd rows of four-sided stitch on seventeenth-century samplers, for example. Mrs. Jackson shows 'Saracenic drawn linen' of about the eleventh century and a German example of the fourteenth century in *History of Lace*, but these are barely more than inventive weaving and the most obvious extant examples of early pulled thread work

172

are Italian of the seventeenth century. These consist of bands where the background is worked in a pulled two-sided Italian cross stitch in colour, leaving the motif plain in the manner of Assisi work. The thread used is invariably silk on a fine or medium-weight linen and the designs vary from well-balanced geometric trees, animals and figures to motifs thrown willy-nilly on to the area of the band regardless of scale or balance, but often amusing and gay in their naïveté. The colour of thread is always rich: deep red, dark rose and dark green are common examples, and the stitching is completely regular, covering the whole background; only a little back stitch is used for detail on the motifs and occasionally as an outline. The stitching is not worked entirely in one direction, as both vertical and horizontal rows are worked, depending on the shape of the area to be filled. There are examples where double faggot stitch forms the background in similar designs. The original purpose of these bands and borders appears to have been lost because they have obviously been part of larger items, possibly for church linen, as an altar cover exists with a similar border but in another method of embroidery.

It is interesting that two-sided Italian cross stitch was then pulled very tightly, whereas now we consider it a canvas-work stitch, which suggests that other counted thread stitches could readily be interchangeable, simply by regulating the tension.

Another surprising form of pulled thread dating from the seventeenth or eighteenth century is shown in examples in the Benaki Museum in Athens; they at first appear to be lacis but on closer inspection show single or double faggot stitch used as a background on fairly fine linen on which some of the ground threads may have been removed to give a more open effect. Large panels and smaller items have been worked in this way and are further enriched either by darning with thick thread into the remaining material or by embroidering the motifs left in material with cross and chain stitches in colour.

During the eighteenth century in Western Europe, that is, in France, Germany, Denmark, Britain and the Low Countries, pulled thread truly became a technique in its own right. Although it plainly began as an imitation of lace it flowered into an original technique requiring a great deal of expertise. Lace-making is constructing a complete fabric from interwoven, knotted or needleworked threads, whereas pulled work began with a fine material which had its texture changed with stitchery. Its origins must also have been fostered by the fact that fine materials were readily available and became an important part of fashion. Some of these materials have names which we still use, cambric meaning a fine French linen, and lawn, which was also a fine linen, but others have quite unfamiliar names; jaconet, a slight soft muslin; nainsook, a Bengal muslin; sleasey, a flimsy silesian lawn and also selesie lawn, meaning a cambric from Silesia. In 1795 'cambric for ruffles' was 10s a yard and a man's handkerchief was 12s, both presumably embroidered at that price, and in 1795 'real India muslins' were from 6d to £1 16s per yard. From these delicate materials a variety of articles were made such as decorative aprons, fichus (then called handkerchiefs) and sleeve falls of which there are many extant examples.

Surprisingly it is very difficult to find examples of babies' clothes in pulled thread of this time, although there are many of Ayrshire embroidery which evolved from pulled thread, so that it can only be concluded that either they were made but due to wear and tear have been lost, or that the delicate materials were not considered suitable for babies' clothes in those days.

There is a baby's bonnet of the mid-eighteenth century in the Bath Museum of Costume, made of fine linen and embroidered in Italian quilting and trapunto with one layer cut away in places to allow a few pulled thread fillings; although charming to look at, the bumpy surfaces must have made it singularly uncomfortable for the baby to wear. The same museum has on show both men's and women's clothes worked with pulled thread, and one or two unusual pieces like a judge's 'lace' cuffs of 1730 which are beautifully worked, and a man's handkerchief which suggest that pulled thread was widely used in the eighteenth century.

During this century richly embroidered clothes for men were fashionable, mainly waistcoats and top coats, and there are quite a number of white twill waistcoats extant combining quilting, rich surface stitchery and pulled thread. It would appear that the quilting was worked first and then the twill was cut away in places so that the pulled thread fillings could be worked on the layer of backing linen. On one or two waistcoats it seems that the fillings are actually worked successfully on twill, which is about the most unsuitable material for the method. Hand-embroidered buttons were requisite to complete these handsome garments; the buttons were made over wooden moulds and, incidentally, if trimmed with french knots were called 'snails', but most unfairly the wearing of covered buttons was made illegal by Acts of both Anne and George I – probably fines were a good source of income from such a popular fashion!

Now to consider the items of dress in detail. Fichus, then called 'handkerchiefs', were of a triangular shape with the point at centre back and the two ends tucked under the front lacing on the bodice, making a soft frame for neck and face and covering the décolletage, and were not 'dress wear'. In *The Guardian* of 1713 a gentleman avers that 'when she [his wife] is at home she is continually muffled up and concealed in mobs [mob caps], morning gowns and handkerchiefs, but strips every afternoon to appear in public'. Perhaps this explains the dearth of portraits of this period illustrating pulled work fichus or sleeve falls; people would want to be painted in their best clothes to which there would have been real lace trimmings, and their Dresden or Tonder worked muslins would perhaps have been considered less impressive.

Tonder in Denmark produced a range of laces from as early as 1647 but was particularly noted for 'Tonder work' during the eighteenth century, which consists of extremely fine pulled thread fillings contained in elaborate floral designs worked on lawn or cambric. 'Dresden work' was in a similar style and both the Whitworth Art Gallery in Manchester and the Victoria and Albert Museum in London have superb German samplers of this time, the Manchester one being described as having been 'worked in a Rhenish nunnery'. Both are divided into many squares and in the London sampler the worker shows an incredible number of different fillings, worked so finely that it is necessary to look at them under a magnifying glass to fully appreciate their expertise and virtuosity, in a combination of stitchery and fabric exhibiting a wide selection of delicate textures. Evidently the fame of Dresden work was far spread, as there is a reference to being taught Dresden work in Anna Winslow's *Diary of a Boston Schoolgirl* of 1773; *American Needlework* mentions French émigrés who '. . . found solace and sometimes sustenance in teaching the fine art of white work they had learned in their youth' and in the same book there is an illustration of a white embroidered mull handkerchief of 1824 which undoubtedly contains skilful pulled work.

The points of the eighteenth-century fichus were usually richly embroidered with pulled fillings, as were the shorter edges of the triangle, although some have only edgings; sleeve falls, which could be in one, two or three gathered layers of fabric, were also embroidered with edgings of varying widths and were cut shorter on the inside of the elbow than on the outside so that in wear they fell in graceful folds revealing both sides of the embroidery.

Aprons were in fashion throughout the century, and were often embroidered in coloured silks or made of rich materials, but muslin or lawn aprons were also popular though fashion decreed that they were longer than other aprons, reaching almost to the ankle, and were purely decorative. There are examples of aprons richly embroidered with pulled work, but more often the work is slight with tamboured outlines of chain stitch enclosing only a few small areas of the simpler pulled thread fillings, such as single faggot, and rarely contain any of the skill and inventiveness shown on the more elaborately worked fichus. In the Folk Museum in Athens a square scarf of muslin on a national costume is designed and worked in an almost identical way to the aprons, but the link is too tenuous for us to be able to draw any conclusion.

The embroiderers of the eighteenth century, more often professional than amateur, intuitively understood the relationship of textures by contrasting smooth outlines of satin stitch, a flat wide buttonhole stitch or chain stitch with the broken textures of fillings, and thereby achieved a harmonious balance; shadow work was sometimes combined with pulled thread fillings as a more subtle textural contrast. The thread used for pulled thread fillings was fine and twisted, and some thread is incredibly fine considering that the methods of spinning were primitive compared with the mechanisation of this century, when paradoxically it is increasingly difficult to obtain strong, fine embroidery thread.

Pulled work on men's twill waistcoats was in quite a contrasting style to the fine work of ladies' clothes, being bold and balanced against quilting and surface stitchery worked in thickish thread; the effect is of shading using depth of texture rather than colour. A bold stylised floral design from shoulder to hem either side of the front opening would be thickly worked, using a range of thread thickness, some of the thread being glossy and some matt. There are unusual combinations of techniques, varying slightly from garment to garment, and pulled work fillings can be seen with surface stitches such as French knots and laid fillings, quilting (both English and trapunto) and round eyelets. Although the majority of articles showing this flamboyant mixture are waistcoats, in the Victoria and Albert Museum they have examples of a stomacher and underskirt and at Gawthorpe Hall an unfinished coverlet.

As embroiderers we have had a tendency to keep embroidery techniques strictly separated, but the modern argument for integrating a variety of methods experimentally is here seen illustrated by our predecessors as visually acceptable, and is found to be valid for practical articles and not only decorative items.

Gradually fashion advanced and other garments came into vogue, changing the style of decoration so that pulled fillings became less and less used while satin stitch was emphasised and eventually broderie Anglaise evolved at the beginning of the nineteenth century.

The eighteenth century has provided us with many examples of Western European dress where pulled work appears in consistent styles, but during the nineteenth and early twentieth centuries it resumes its chameleon quality and there are examples from such countries as Russia, India, Greece, Czechoslovakia, Spain, Turkey, Sicily and South America, showing mainly a use of the simpler fillings combined with other techniques. There are particularly interesting examples from Russia and the Greek Islands where single or double faggot stitch is worked as a bold background on coarse linen, leaving the design in plain material; the designs are simple and naïve in peasant tradition, but because of their vigour and straightforward approach are extremely effective. The articles made are invariably household linen, of which a buffet cloth is illustrated, and are sturdily made with a view to hard wear.

Nowadays Scandinavian countries are well known for their peasant tradition of attractive counted thread work, which includes much pulled thread and is successful in both geometric and figurative design simply because it is unpretentious and based on an inborn appreciation of scale and texture in combining stitches, thread and fabric. There is little point in trying to emulate the peasant tradition if we have been brought up in the sophisticated industrial environment of modern countries, but we can try to embroider with their honesty of approach. Historical work teaches us that each age has been unconsciously influenced by trends in fashion and décor, by trade and wars affecting the availability of threads and materials and by other apparently extraneous influences. Embroidery should reflect the age in which it is worked in the same way as art, fashion, furniture and other crafts; experiment is essential to counteract a stagnation of ideas and must needs result in some work of a high aesthetic value.

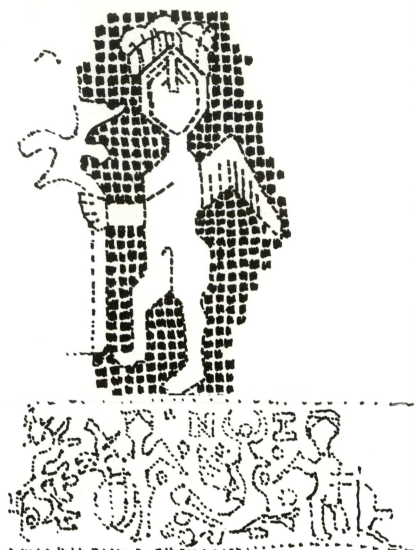

Italian seventeenth century. This angel forms the basis of the repetitive border together with an exotic bird and plant motif and the initials N.I. The background of the border, which is about 4″ (10 cm) wide, is in two-sided Italian cross stitch. (By kind permission of the Victoria and Albert Museum.)

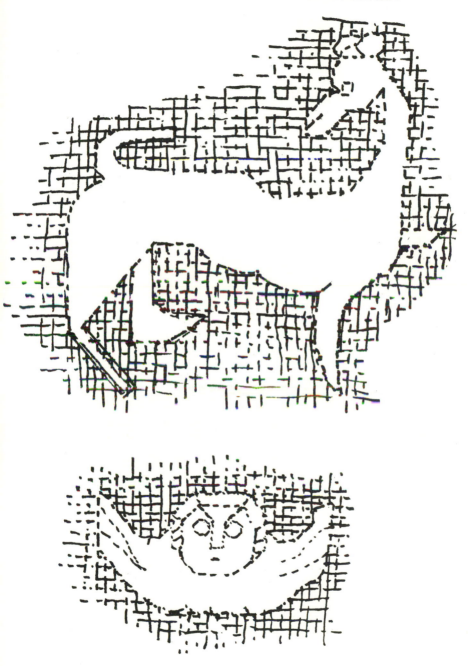

Three motifs from a border about 6″ (15 cm) wide
where animals, snakes, griffons and cherubs are shown
arranged haphazardly in a repeated design. The
background is in fine two-sided Italian cross stitch in
deep rose-pink silk thread. (By kind permission of the
Victoria and Albert Museum.)

Opposite:
Italian seventeenth century. A crisply designed oak
tree forms the motif for a repeating vertical border.
The background and outlines within the design are
two-sided Italian cross stitch in strawberry-pink twisted
silk on white linen. The designer has shown
understanding of the technique as the stitches fit easily
into the stylised shapes. (By kind permission of the
Whitworth Art Gallery, University of Manchester.)

182

Italian seventeenth century. A competent, professional-looking border, heraldic in style. The design has obviously been made specifically for this width of border. Rust-red two-sided Italian cross stitch forms the background. (By kind permission of the Victoria and Albert Museum.)
Overleaf left:
Leucas, Ionian Islands. Seventeenth/eighteenth century. This is a colourful, richly embroidered hanging although the motifs themselves are primitive in design. The background is in single faggot stitch and the figures are embroidered in red, green, and orange in cross and chain stitches. (By kind permission of the Benaki Museum, Athens.)

Overleaf right:
At first sight it would seem likely that this panel had
come from Scandinavia rather than the Dodecanese by
the style of design, in its fresh simplicity and
understanding of designing within the limitations of the
counted thread technique. Some threads were probably
removed before working the background in double
faggot stitch to give a more open effect, and then a
thickish thread was used to emphasise the motifs with
darning or double running stitch. The face shows how,
with a minimum of detail, features, character and
expression can be suggested. Seventeenth or eighteenth
century. (By kind permission of the Benaki Museum,
Athens.)

185

cap.

Silk
brocade
dress.

fichu (handkerchief)
shallow point at
back.

Sleeve fall

Apron

This is a sketch to show articles of dress that were
embroidered with pulled work as they would have
appeared in wear, about the middle of the eighteenth
century in England.

This drawing is of an elaborate motif worked in the
point of a fichu and containing a wide variety of
fillings, outlined with chain stitch and buttonhole

189

stitch. It dates from the first half of the eighteenth
century. (By kind permission of the City of Liverpool
Museum.)

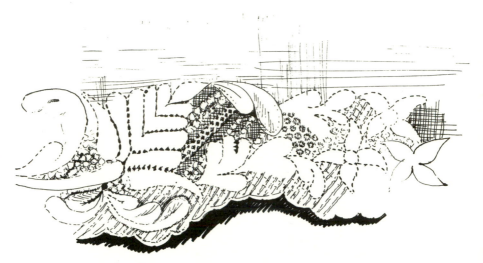

Border from the edge of a fichu very finely
embroidered in shadow work and pulled thread fillings,
about actual size. (By kind permission of the City of
Liverpool Museum.)

Opposite:
Basic floral design from a sleeve fall with an elaborate
scalloped edge; the outlines are either button-holed or
chain-stitched and enclose a variety of fillings.
Eighteenth century. (By kind permission of Liverpool
City Museum.)

190

Basic design from the corner of a muslin apron worked
mainly in chain stitch as the design, although pretty,
provides for only small areas of pulled fillings in the
floral shapes and scalloped edge. Eighteenth century.
(By kind permission of the City of Liverpool Museum.)

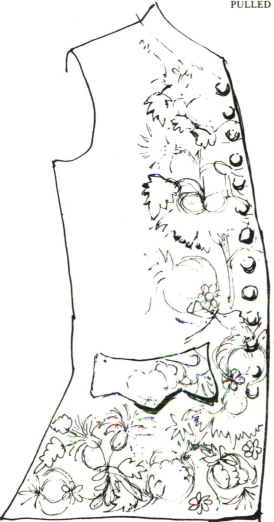

Gentleman's twill waistcoat of 1760–70 lined with
linen; the whole design is richly embroidered in
off-white in a mixture of techniques, including pulled
work. The pocket flap is purely decorative and it is
quite possible that some of the buttons, embroidered
with a satin stitch star, were never intended to enter
the many buttonholes. (By kind permission of the City
of Liverpool Museum.)

Opposite:
Part of the basic design of the embroidery on the
preceding waistcoat showing the bold floral shapes
based on carnations, pomegranates and forget-me-nots.

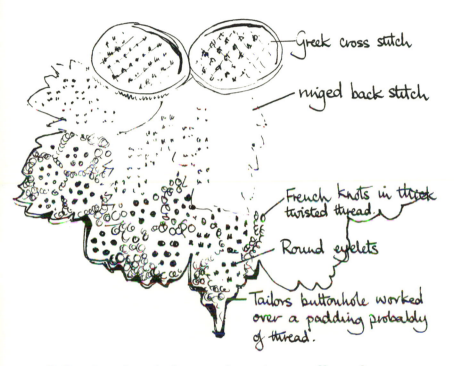

Greek cross stitch

ringed back stitch

French knots in thick
twisted thread.

Round eyelets

Tailors buttonhole worked
over a padding probably
of thread.

Detail showing the stitches used to give an effect of
shading with depth of texture rather than colour, on
the preceding waistcoat.

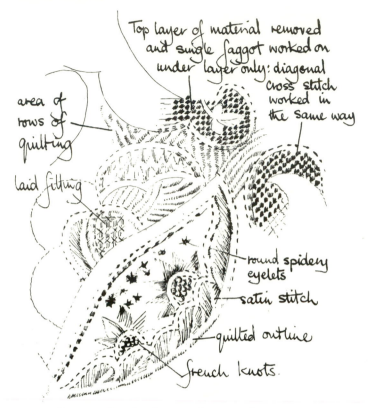

Top layer of material removed and single faggot worked on under layer only: diagonal cross stitch worked in the same way

area of rows of quilting

laid filling

round spidery eyelets

satin stitch

quilted outline

french knots.

Part of an unfinished coverlet combining a variety of techniques. (By kind permission of the trustees of Gawthorpe Hall.)

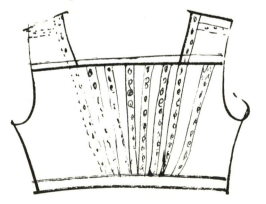

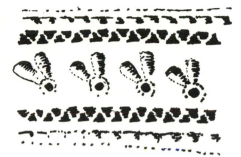

Opposite below:
Sketch of an Empire chemisette at Gawthorpe Hall
which is skilfully shaped by inserting bands of
embroidery between crossway cut sections. The above
insertion shows satin stitch, round eyelets, single rows
of honeycomb stitch and a pulled back stitch, and
demonstrates in a small way the transition between
the pulled work of the eighteenth century and broderie
Anglaise.

Overleaf:
Russian early nineteenth century. This is the wide
border of a buffet cloth of formal motifs outlined very
boldly in two rows of chain stitch in a thick thread,
giving an almost sculptured appearance against the
background of single faggot. The round eyelets are
rather inexpertly executed, but the whole piece has
great vigour and is on a suitably bold scale for a large
cloth which might well have been viewed across a large
room. (By kind permission of the Whitworth Art
Gallery, University of Manchester.)

197

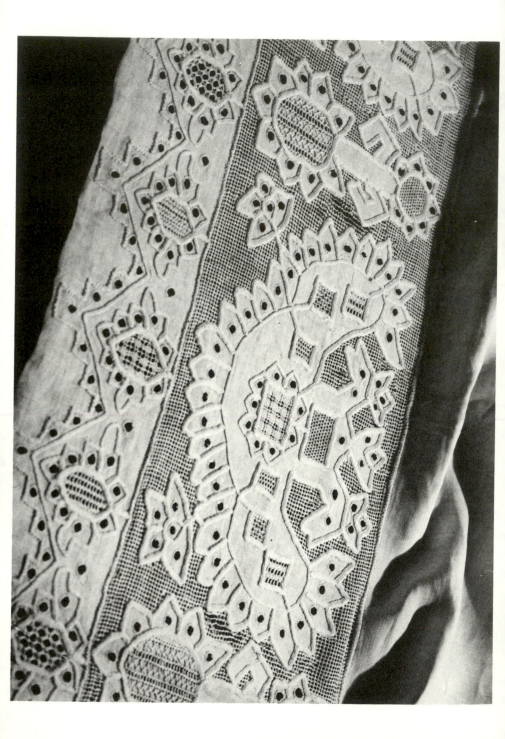

Another wide band forming a frieze of animal, ship and human motifs in a strong peasant tradition. The background is worked in double faggot stitch on a coarse cotton ground and the whole is described as a bed edge. (Greek, probably this century, in the Wace Collection at Liverpool City Museum.)

Overleaf left:
Part of a German eighteenth-century sampler illustrating the skill and inventiveness of the worker. (By courtesy of the Victoria and Albert Museum.)

Overleaf right:
A mat worked in Germany in 1937 shows the same high standard of technical skill as in the eighteenth century. (The Needlework Development Scheme collection at the Embroiderers' Guild.)

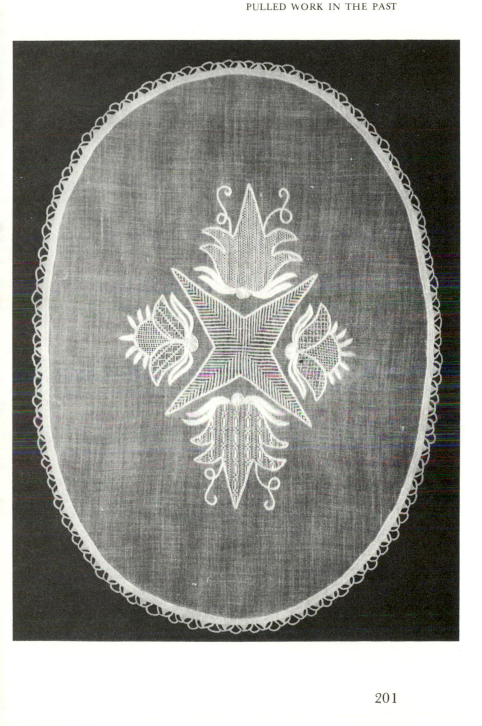

Part of the front panel from an unfinished christening
robe of the nineteenth century. The figures, mainly in
French knots and trailing, stand out against a
background of single faggot stitch. (The Needlework
Development Scheme collection at the Embroiderers'
Guild.)

202

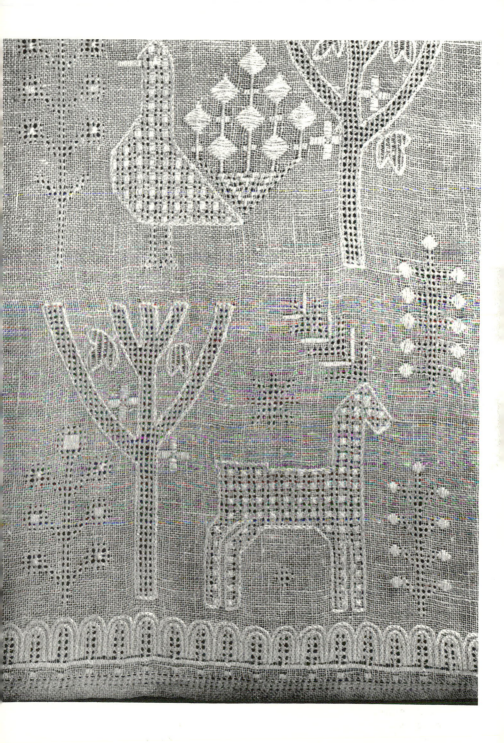

Previous page:
An attractive Swedish cloth of 1947 shows simply
shaped and worked motifs on a thick, rich linen.
Four-sided stitch and satin stitch with chain-stitch
outlining are the main stitches used. (The Needlework
Development Scheme collection at the Embroiderers'
Guild.)

Overleaf:
A deceptively simple design on a Norwegian mat of
1949, based on the change of stitch direction. Astrid
Sandvold. (The Needlework Development Scheme
collection at the Embroiderers' Guild.)

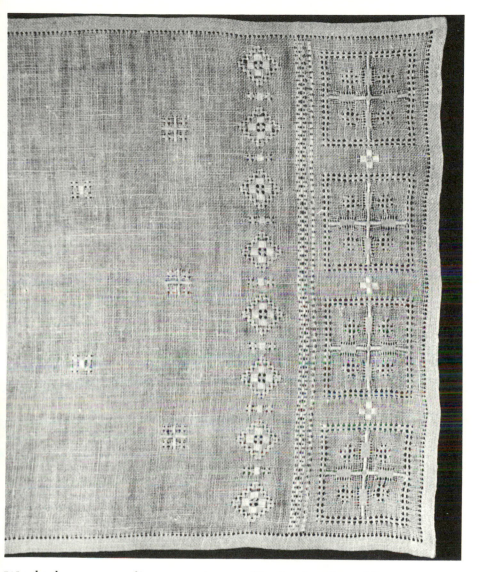

Worked on a grey linen mat is an effective border with
spot motifs to decorate the centre; note how the spots
are varied to avoid tedium. Svensk Hemslojd, 1948,
Sweden. (The Needlework Development Scheme
collection at the Embroiderers' Guild.)

BIBLIOGRAPHY

Illustrated English Social History: 3   G. M. Trevelyan.
History of Lace   Mrs. F. Nevill Jackson.*
Handbook of English Costume   G. W. and P. Cunnington.
American Needlework   Georgiana Brown Harbeson.
Diary of a Boston Schoolgirl   ed. Alice Morse Earle.
Hungarian Domestic Embroidery   Maria Varju.

*Reprinted by Dover as *Old Handmade Lace: With a Dictionary of Lace.*

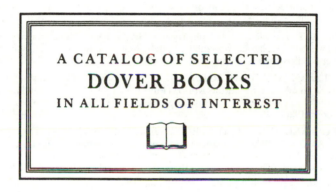

A CATALOG OF SELECTED

DOVER BOOKS

IN ALL FIELDS OF INTEREST

A CATALOG OF SELECTED DOVER
BOOKS IN ALL FIELDS OF INTEREST

CONCERNING THE SPIRITUAL IN ART, Wassily Kandinsky. Pioneering work by father of abstract art. Thoughts on color theory, nature of art. Analysis of earlier masters. 12 illustrations. 80pp. of text. 5⅜ x 8½.   0-486-23411-8

CELTIC ART: The Methods of Construction, George Bain. Simple geometric techniques for making Celtic interlacements, spirals, Kells-type initials, animals, humans, etc. Over 500 illustrations. 160pp. 9 x 12. (Available in U.S. only.)   0-486-22923-8

AN ATLAS OF ANATOMY FOR ARTISTS, Fritz Schider. Most thorough reference work on art anatomy in the world. Hundreds of illustrations, including selections from works by Vesalius, Leonardo, Goya, Ingres, Michelangelo, others. 593 illustrations. 192pp. 7⅛ x 10¼.   0-486-20241-0

CELTIC HAND STROKE-BY-STROKE (Irish Half-Uncial from "The Book of Kells"): An Arthur Baker Calligraphy Manual, Arthur Baker. Complete guide to creating each letter of the alphabet in distinctive Celtic manner. Covers hand position, strokes, pens, inks, paper, more. Illustrated. 48pp. 8¼ x 11.   0-486-24336-2

EASY ORIGAMI, John Montroll. Charming collection of 32 projects (hat, cup, pelican, piano, swan, many more) specially designed for the novice origami hobbyist. Clearly illustrated easy-to-follow instructions insure that even beginning papercrafters will achieve successful results. 48pp. 8¼ x 11.   0-486-27298-2

BLOOMINGDALE'S ILLUSTRATED 1886 CATALOG: Fashions, Dry Goods and Housewares, Bloomingdale Brothers. Famed merchants' extremely rare catalog depicting about 1,700 products: clothing, housewares, firearms, dry goods, jewelry, more. Invaluable for dating, identifying vintage items. Also, copyright-free graphics for artists, designers. Co-published with Henry Ford Museum & Greenfield Village. 160pp. 8¼ x 11.   0-486-25780-0

THE ART OF WORLDLY WISDOM, Baltasar Gracian. "Think with the few and speak with the many," "Friends are a second existence," and "Be able to forget" are among this 1637 volume's 300 pithy maxims. A perfect source of mental and spiritual refreshment, it can be opened at random and appreciated either in brief or at length. 128pp. 5⅜ x 8½.   0-486-44034-6

JOHNSON'S DICTIONARY: A Modern Selection, Samuel Johnson (E. L. McAdam and George Milne, eds.). This modern version reduces the original 1755 edition's 2,300 pages of definitions and literary examples to a more manageable length, retaining the verbal pleasure and historical curiosity of the original. 480pp. 5³⁄₁₆ x 8¼.   0-486-44089-3

ADVENTURES OF HUCKLEBERRY FINN, Mark Twain, Illustrated by E. W. Kemble. A work of eternal richness and complexity, a source of ongoing critical debate, and a literary landmark, Twain's 1885 masterpiece about a barefoot boy's journey of self-discovery has enthralled readers around the world. This handsome clothbound reproduction of the first edition features all 174 of the original black-and-white illustrations. 368pp. 5⅜ x 8½.   0-486-44322-1

STICKLEY CRAFTSMAN FURNITURE CATALOGS, Gustav Stickley and L. & J. G. Stickley. Beautiful, functional furniture in two authentic catalogs from 1910. 594 illustrations, including 277 photos, show settles, rockers, armchairs, reclining chairs, bookcases, desks, tables. 183pp. 6½ x 9¼.   0-486-23838-5

AMERICAN LOCOMOTIVES IN HISTORIC PHOTOGRAPHS: 1858 to 1949, Ron Ziel (ed.). A rare collection of 126 meticulously detailed official photographs, called "builder portraits," of American locomotives that majestically chronicle the rise of steam locomotive power in America. Introduction. Detailed captions. xi+ 129pp. 9 x 12.   0-486-27393-8

AMERICA'S LIGHTHOUSES: An Illustrated History, Francis Ross Holland, Jr. Delightfully written, profusely illustrated fact-filled survey of over 200 American lighthouses since 1716. History, anecdotes, technological advances, more. 240pp. 8 x 10¾.
                                    0-486-25576-X

TOWARDS A NEW ARCHITECTURE, Le Corbusier. Pioneering manifesto by founder of "International School." Technical and aesthetic theories, views of industry, economics, relation of form to function, "mass-production split" and much more. Profusely illustrated. 320pp. 6⅛ x 9¼. (Available in U.S. only.)   0-486-25023-7

HOW THE OTHER HALF LIVES, Jacob Riis. Famous journalistic record, exposing poverty and degradation of New York slums around 1900, by major social reformer. 100 striking and influential photographs. 233pp. 10 x 7⅞.   0-486-22012-5

FRUIT KEY AND TWIG KEY TO TREES AND SHRUBS, William M. Harlow. One of the handiest and most widely used identification aids. Fruit key covers 120 deciduous and evergreen species; twig key 160 deciduous species. Easily used. Over 300 photographs. 126pp. 5⅜ x 8½.   0-486-20511-8

COMMON BIRD SONGS, Dr. Donald J. Borror. Songs of 60 most common U.S. birds: robins, sparrows, cardinals, bluejays, finches, more—arranged in order of increasing complexity. Up to 9 variations of songs of each species.
                                    Cassette and manual 0-486-99911-4

ORCHIDS AS HOUSE PLANTS, Rebecca Tyson Northen. Grow cattleyas and many other kinds of orchids—in a window, in a case, or under artificial light. 63 illustrations. 148pp. 5⅜ x 8½.   0-486-23261-1

MONSTER MAZES, Dave Phillips. Masterful mazes at four levels of difficulty. Avoid deadly perils and evil creatures to find magical treasures. Solutions for all 32 exciting illustrated puzzles. 48pp. 8¼ x 11.   0-486-26005-4

MOZART'S DON GIOVANNI (DOVER OPERA LIBRETTO SERIES), Wolfgang Amadeus Mozart. Introduced and translated by Ellen H. Bleiler. Standard Italian libretto, with complete English translation. Convenient and thoroughly portable—an ideal companion for reading along with a recording or the performance itself. Introduction. List of characters. Plot summary. 121pp. 5¼ x 8½.   0-486-24944-1

FRANK LLOYD WRIGHT'S DANA HOUSE, Donald Hoffmann. Pictorial essay of residential masterpiece with over 160 interior and exterior photos, plans, elevations, sketches and studies. 128pp. 9¼ x 10¾.   0-486-29120-0

THE CLARINET AND CLARINET PLAYING, David Pino. Lively, comprehensive work features suggestions about technique, musicianship, and musical interpretation, as well as guidelines for teaching, making your own reeds, and preparing for public performance. Includes an intriguing look at clarinet history. "A godsend," *The Clarinet,* Journal of the International Clarinet Society. Appendixes. 7 illus. 320pp. 5⅜ x 8½. 0-486-40270-3

HOLLYWOOD GLAMOR PORTRAITS, John Kobal (ed.). 145 photos from 1926-49. Harlow, Gable, Bogart, Bacall; 94 stars in all. Full background on photographers, technical aspects. 160pp. 8⅜ x 11¼. 0-486-23352-9

THE RAVEN AND OTHER FAVORITE POEMS, Edgar Allan Poe. Over 40 of the author's most memorable poems: "The Bells," "Ulalume," "Israfel," "To Helen," "The Conqueror Worm," "Eldorado," "Annabel Lee," many more. Alphabetic lists of titles and first lines. 64pp. 5³⁄₁₆ x 8¼. 0-486-26685-0

PERSONAL MEMOIRS OF U. S. GRANT, Ulysses Simpson Grant. Intelligent, deeply moving firsthand account of Civil War campaigns, considered by many the finest military memoirs ever written. Includes letters, historic photographs, maps and more. 528pp. 6⅛ x 9¼. 0-486-28587-1

POE ILLUSTRATED: Art by Doré, Dulac, Rackham and Others, selected and edited by Jeff A. Menges. More than 100 compelling illustrations, in brilliant color and crisp black-and-white, include scenes from "The Raven," "The Pit and the Pendulum," "The Gold-Bug," and other stories and poems. 96pp. 8⅜ x 11. 0-486-45746-X

RUSSIAN STORIES/RUSSKIE RASSKAZY: A Dual-Language Book, edited by Gleb Struve. Twelve tales by such masters as Chekhov, Tolstoy, Dostoevsky, Pushkin, others. Excellent word-for-word English translations on facing pages, plus teaching and study aids, Russian/English vocabulary, biographical/critical introductions, more. 416pp. 5⅜ x 8½. 0-486-26244-8

PHILADELPHIA THEN AND NOW: 60 Sites Photographed in the Past and Present, Kenneth Finkel and Susan Oyama. Rare photographs of City Hall, Logan Square, Independence Hall, Betsy Ross House, other landmarks juxtaposed with contemporary views. Captures changing face of historic city. Introduction. Captions. 128pp. 8¼ x 11. 0-486-25790-8

NORTH AMERICAN INDIAN LIFE: Customs and Traditions of 23 Tribes, Elsie Clews Parsons (ed.). 27 fictionalized essays by noted anthropologists examine religion, customs, government, additional facets of life among the Winnebago, Crow, Zuni, Eskimo, other tribes. 480pp. 6⅛ x 9¼. 0-486-27377-6

TECHNICAL MANUAL AND DICTIONARY OF CLASSICAL BALLET, Gail Grant. Defines, explains, comments on steps, movements, poses and concepts. 15-page pictorial section. Basic book for student, viewer. 127pp. 5⅜ x 8½. 0-486-21843-0

THE MALE AND FEMALE FIGURE IN MOTION: 60 Classic Photographic Sequences, Eadweard Muybridge. 60 true-action photographs of men and women walking, running, climbing, bending, turning, etc., reproduced from a rare 19th-century masterpiece. vi + 121pp. 9 x 12. 0-486-24745-7

ANIMALS: 1,419 Copyright-Free Illustrations of Mammals, Birds, Fish, Insects, etc., Jim Harter (ed.). Clear wood engravings present, in extremely lifelike poses, over 1,000 species of animals. One of the most extensive pictorial sourcebooks of its kind. Captions. Index. 284pp. 9 x 12. 0-486-23766-4

1001 QUESTIONS ANSWERED ABOUT THE SEASHORE, N. J. Berrill and Jacquelyn Berrill. Queries answered about dolphins, sea snails, sponges, starfish, fishes, shore birds, many others. Covers appearance, breeding, growth, feeding, much more. 305pp. 5¼ x 8¼. 0-486-23366-9

ATTRACTING BIRDS TO YOUR YARD, William J. Weber. Easy-to-follow guide offers advice on how to attract the greatest diversity of birds: birdhouses, feeders, water and waterers, much more. 96pp. 5³⁄₁₆ x 8¼. 0-486-28927-3

MEDICINAL AND OTHER USES OF NORTH AMERICAN PLANTS: A Historical Survey with Special Reference to the Eastern Indian Tribes, Charlotte Erichsen-Brown. Chronological historical citations document 500 years of usage of plants, trees, shrubs native to eastern Canada, northeastern U.S. Also complete identifying information. 343 illustrations. 544pp. 6½ x 9¼. 0-486-25951-X

STORYBOOK MAZES, Dave Phillips. 23 stories and mazes on two-page spreads: Wizard of Oz, Treasure Island, Robin Hood, etc. Solutions. 64pp. 8¼ x 11.
0-486-23628-5

AMERICAN NEGRO SONGS: 230 Folk Songs and Spirituals, Religious and Secular, John W. Work. This authoritative study traces the African influences of songs sung and played by black Americans at work, in church, and as entertainment. The author discusses the lyric significance of such songs as "Swing Low, Sweet Chariot," "John Henry," and others and offers the words and music for 230 songs. Bibliography. Index of Song Titles. 272pp. 6½ x 9¼. 0-486-40271-1

MOVIE-STAR PORTRAITS OF THE FORTIES, John Kobal (ed.). 163 glamor, studio photos of 106 stars of the 1940s: Rita Hayworth, Ava Gardner, Marlon Brando, Clark Gable, many more. 176pp. 8⅜ x 11¼. 0-486-23546-7

YEKL and THE IMPORTED BRIDEGROOM AND OTHER STORIES OF YIDDISH NEW YORK, Abraham Cahan. Film Hester Street based on Yekl (1896). Novel, other stories among first about Jewish immigrants on N.Y.'s East Side. 240pp. 5⅜ x 8½. 0-486-22427-9

SELECTED POEMS, Walt Whitman. Generous sampling from Leaves of Grass. Twenty-four poems include "I Hear America Singing," "Song of the Open Road," "I Sing the Body Electric," "When Lilacs Last in the Dooryard Bloom'd," "O Captain! My Captain!"—all reprinted from an authoritative edition. Lists of titles and first lines. 128pp. 5³⁄₁₆ x 8¼. 0-486-26878-0

SONGS OF EXPERIENCE: Facsimile Reproduction with 26 Plates in Full Color, William Blake. 26 full-color plates from a rare 1826 edition. Includes "The Tyger," "London," "Holy Thursday," and other poems. Printed text of poems. 48pp. 5¼ x 7.
0-486-24636-1

THE BEST TALES OF HOFFMANN, E. T. A. Hoffmann. 10 of Hoffmann's most important stories: "Nutcracker and the King of Mice," "The Golden Flowerpot," etc. 458pp. 5⅜ x 8½. 0-486-21793-0

THE BOOK OF TEA, Kakuzo Okakura. Minor classic of the Orient: entertaining, charming explanation, interpretation of traditional Japanese culture in terms of tea ceremony. 94pp. 5⅜ x 8½. 0-486-20070-1

FRENCH STORIES/CONTES FRANÇAIS: A Dual-Language Book, Wallace Fowlie. Ten stories by French masters, Voltaire to Camus: "Micromegas" by Voltaire; "The Atheist's Mass" by Balzac; "Minuet" by de Maupassant; "The Guest" by Camus, six more. Excellent English translations on facing pages. Also French-English vocabulary list, exercises, more. 352pp. 5⅜ x 8½. 0-486-26443-2

CHICAGO AT THE TURN OF THE CENTURY IN PHOTOGRAPHS: 122 Historic Views from the Collections of the Chicago Historical Society, Larry A. Viskochil. Rare large-format prints offer detailed views of City Hall, State Street, the Loop, Hull House, Union Station, many other landmarks, circa 1904-1913. Introduction. Captions. Maps. 144pp. 9⅜ x 12¼. 0-486-24656-6

OLD BROOKLYN IN EARLY PHOTOGRAPHS, 1865–1929, William Lee Younger. Luna Park, Gravesend race track, construction of Grand Army Plaza, moving of Hotel Brighton, etc. 157 previously unpublished photographs. 165pp. 8⅞ x 11¾. 0-486-23587-4

THE MYTHS OF THE NORTH AMERICAN INDIANS, Lewis Spence. Rich anthology of the myths and legends of the Algonquins, Iroquois, Pawnees and Sioux, prefaced by an extensive historical and ethnological commentary. 36 illustrations. 480pp. 5⅜ x 8½. 0-486-25967-6

AN ENCYCLOPEDIA OF BATTLES: Accounts of Over 1,560 Battles from 1479 B.C. to the Present, David Eggenberger. Essential details of every major battle in recorded history from the first battle of Megiddo in 1479 B.C. to Grenada in 1984. List of Battle Maps. New Appendix covering the years 1967–1984. Index. 99 illustrations. 544pp. 6½ x 9¼. 0-486-24913-1

SAILING ALONE AROUND THE WORLD, Captain Joshua Slocum. First man to sail around the world, alone, in small boat. One of the great feats of seamanship told in delightful manner. 67 illustrations. 294pp. 5⅜ x 8½. 0-486-20326-3

ANARCHISM AND OTHER ESSAYS, Emma Goldman. Powerful, penetrating, prophetic essays on direct action, role of minorities, prison reform, puritan hypocrisy, violence, etc. 271pp. 5⅜ x 8½. 0-486-22484-8

MYTHS OF THE HINDUS AND BUDDHISTS, Ananda K. Coomaraswamy and Sister Nivedita. Great stories of the epics; deeds of Krishna, Shiva, taken from puranas, Vedas, folk tales; etc. 32 illustrations. 400pp. 5⅜ x 8½. 0-486-21759-0

MY BONDAGE AND MY FREEDOM, Frederick Douglass. Born a slave, Douglass became outspoken force in antislavery movement. The best of Douglass' autobiographies. Graphic description of slave life. 464pp. 5⅜ x 8½. 0-486-22457-0

FOLLOWING THE EQUATOR: A Journey Around the World, Mark Twain. Fascinating humorous account of 1897 voyage to Hawaii, Australia, India, New Zealand, etc. Ironic, bemused reports on peoples, customs, climate, flora and fauna, politics, much more. 197 illustrations. 720pp. 5⅜ x 8½. 0-486-26113-1

GREAT SPEECHES BY AMERICAN WOMEN, edited by James Daley. Here are 21 legendary speeches from the country's most inspirational female voices, including Sojourner Truth, Susan B. Anthony, Eleanor Roosevelt, Hillary Rodham Clinton, Nancy Pelosi, and many others. 192pp. 5³⁄₁₆ x 8¼. 0-486-46141-6

THE MYTHS OF GREECE AND ROME, H. A. Guerber. A classic of mythology, generously illustrated, long prized for its simple, graphic, accurate retelling of the principal myths of Greece and Rome, and for its commentary on their origins and significance. With 64 illustrations by Michelangelo, Raphael, Titian, Rubens, Canova, Bernini and others. 480pp. 5⅜ x 8½. 0-486-27584-1

PSYCHOLOGY OF MUSIC, Carl E. Seashore. Classic work discusses music as a medium from psychological viewpoint. Clear treatment of physical acoustics, auditory apparatus, sound perception, development of musical skills, nature of musical feeling, host of other topics. 88 figures. 408pp. 5⅜ x 8½. 0-486-21851-1

LIFE IN ANCIENT EGYPT, Adolf Erman. Fullest, most thorough, detailed older account with much not in more recent books, domestic life, religion, magic, medicine, commerce, much more. Many illustrations reproduce tomb paintings, carvings, hieroglyphs, etc. 597pp. 5⅜ x 8½. 0-486-22632-8

SUNDIALS, Their Theory and Construction, Albert Waugh. Far and away the best, most thorough coverage of ideas, mathematics concerned, types, construction, adjusting anywhere. Simple, nontechnical treatment allows even children to build several of these dials. Over 100 illustrations. 230pp. 5⅜ x 8½. 0-486-22947-5

GREAT SPEECHES BY AFRICAN AMERICANS: Frederick Douglass, Sojourner Truth, Dr. Martin Luther King, Jr., Barack Obama, and Others, edited by James Daley. Tracing the struggle for freedom and civil rights across two centuries, this anthology comprises speeches by Martin Luther King, Jr., Marcus Garvey, Malcolm X, Barack Obama, and many other influential figures. 160pp. 5³⁄₁₆ x 8¼. 0-486-44761-8

OLD-TIME VIGNETTES IN FULL COLOR, Carol Belanger Grafton (ed.). Over 390 charming, often sentimental illustrations, selected from archives of Victorian graphics–pretty women posing, children playing, food, flowers, kittens and puppies, smiling cherubs, birds and butterflies, much more. All copyright-free. 48pp. 9¼ x 12¼. 0-486-27269-9

PERSPECTIVE FOR ARTISTS, Rex Vicat Cole. Depth, perspective of sky and sea, shadows, much more, not usually covered. 391 diagrams, 81 reproductions of drawings and paintings. 279pp. 5⅜ x 8½. 0-486-22487-2

DRAWING THE LIVING FIGURE, Joseph Sheppard. Innovative approach to artistic anatomy focuses on specifics of surface anatomy, rather than muscles and bones. Over 170 drawings of live models in front, back and side views, and in widely varying poses. Accompanying diagrams. 177 illustrations. Introduction. Index. 144pp. 8⅜ x11¼. 0-486-26723-7

GOTHIC AND OLD ENGLISH ALPHABETS: 100 Complete Fonts, Dan X. Solo. Add power, elegance to posters, signs, other graphics with 100 stunning copyright-free alphabets: Blackstone, Dolbey, Germania, 97 more–including many lower-case, numerals, punctuation marks. 104pp. 8⅛ x 11. 0-486-24695-7

THE BOOK OF WOOD CARVING, Charles Marshall Sayers. Finest book for beginners discusses fundamentals and offers 34 designs. "Absolutely first rate . . . well thought out and well executed."–E. J. Tangerman. 118pp. 7¾ x 10⅝. 0-486-23654-4

ILLUSTRATED CATALOG OF CIVIL WAR MILITARY GOODS: Union Army Weapons, Insignia, Uniform Accessories, and Other Equipment, Schuyler, Hartley, and Graham. Rare, profusely illustrated 1846 catalog includes Union Army uniform and dress regulations, arms and ammunition, coats, insignia, flags, swords, rifles, etc. 226 illustrations. 160pp. 9 x 12. 0-486-24939-5

WOMEN'S FASHIONS OF THE EARLY 1900s: An Unabridged Republication of "New York Fashions, 1909," National Cloak & Suit Co. Rare catalog of mail-order fashions documents women's and children's clothing styles shortly after the turn of the century. Captions offer full descriptions, prices. Invaluable resource for fashion, costume historians. Approximately 725 illustrations. 128pp. 8⅜ x 11¼. 0-486-27276-1

HOW TO DO BEADWORK, Mary White. Fundamental book on craft from simple projects to five-bead chains and woven works. 106 illustrations. 142pp. 5⅜ x 8.
0-486-20697-1

THE 1912 AND 1915 GUSTAV STICKLEY FURNITURE CATALOGS, Gustav Stickley. With over 200 detailed illustrations and descriptions, these two catalogs are essential reading and reference materials and identification guides for Stickley furniture. Captions cite materials, dimensions and prices. 112pp. 6½ x 9¼. 0-486-26676-1

SIX GREAT DIALOGUES: Apology, Crito, Phaedo, Phaedrus, Symposium, The Republic, Plato, translated by Benjamin Jowett. Plato's Dialogues rank among Western civilization's most important and influential philosophical works. These 6 selections of his major works explore a broad range of enduringly relevant issues. Authoritative Jowett translations. 480pp. 5³⁄₁₆ x 8¼. 0-486-45465-7

DEMONOLATRY: An Account of the Historical Practice of Witchcraft, Nicolas Remy, edited with an Introduction and Notes by Montague Summers, translated by E. A. Ashwin. This extremely influential 1595 study was frequently cited at witchcraft trials. In addition to lurid details of satanic pacts and sexual perversity, it presents the particulars of numerous court cases. 240pp. 6½ x 9¼. 0-486-46137-8

VICTORIAN FASHIONS AND COSTUMES FROM HARPER'S BAZAAR, 1867–1898, Stella Blum (ed.). Day costumes, evening wear, sports clothes, shoes, hats, other accessories in over 1,000 detailed engravings. 320pp. 9⅜ x 12¼.
0-486-22990-4

THE LONG ISLAND RAIL ROAD IN EARLY PHOTOGRAPHS, Ron Ziel. Over 220 rare photos, informative text document origin (1844) and development of rail service on Long Island. Vintage views of early trains, locomotives, stations, passengers, crews, much more. Captions. 8⅞ x 11¾. 0-486-26301-0

VOYAGE OF THE LIBERDADE, Joshua Slocum. Great 19th-century mariner's thrilling, first-hand account of the wreck of his ship off South America, the 35-foot boat he built from the wreckage, and its remarkable voyage home. 128pp. 5⅜ x 8½.
0-486-40022-0

TEN BOOKS ON ARCHITECTURE, Vitruvius. The most important book ever written on architecture. Early Roman aesthetics, technology, classical orders, site selection, all other aspects. Morgan translation. 331pp. 5⅜ x 8½. 0-486-20645-9

THE HUMAN FIGURE IN MOTION, Eadweard Muybridge. More than 4,500 stopped-action photos, in action series, showing undraped men, women, children jumping, lying down, throwing, sitting, wrestling, carrying, etc. 390pp. 7⅞ x 10⅝.
0-486-20204-6 Clothbd.

TREES OF THE EASTERN AND CENTRAL UNITED STATES AND CANADA, William M. Harlow. Best one-volume guide to 140 trees. Full descriptions, woodlore, range, etc. Over 600 illustrations. Handy size. 288pp. 4½ x 6⅜. 0-486-20395-6

MY FIRST BOOK OF TCHAIKOVSKY: Favorite Pieces in Easy Piano Arrangements, edited by David Dutkanicz. These special arrangements of favorite Tchaikovsky themes are ideal for beginner pianists, child or adult. Contents include themes from "The Nutcracker," "March Slav," Symphonies Nos. 5 and 6, "Swan Lake," "Sleeping Beauty," and more. 48pp. 8¼ x 11. 0-486-46416-4

BIG BOOK OF MAZES AND LABYRINTHS, Walter Shepherd. 50 mazes and labyrinths in all–classical, solid, ripple, and more–in one great volume. Perfect inexpensive puzzler for clever youngsters. Full solutions. 112pp. 8⅛ x 11. 0-486-22951-3

PIANO TUNING, J. Cree Fischer. Clearest, best book for beginner, amateur. Simple repairs, raising dropped notes, tuning by easy method of flattened fifths. No previous skills needed. 4 illustrations. 201pp. 5⅜ x 8½. 0-486-23267-0

CATALOG OF DOVER BOOKS

HINTS TO SINGERS, Lillian Nordica. Selecting the right teacher, developing confidence, overcoming stage fright, and many other important skills receive thoughtful discussion in this indispensible guide, written by a world-famous diva of four decades' experience. 96pp. 5⅜ x 8½. 0-486-40094-8

THE COMPLETE NONSENSE OF EDWARD LEAR, Edward Lear. All nonsense limericks, zany alphabets, Owl and Pussycat, songs, nonsense botany, etc., illustrated by Lear. Total of 320pp. 5⅜ x 8½. (Available in U.S. only.) 0-486-20167-8

VICTORIAN PARLOUR POETRY: An Annotated Anthology, Michael R. Turner. 117 gems by Longfellow, Tennyson, Browning, many lesser-known poets. "The Village Blacksmith," "Curfew Must Not Ring Tonight," "Only a Baby Small," dozens more, often difficult to find elsewhere. Index of poets, titles, first lines. xxiii + 325pp. 5⅜ x 8¼. 0-486-27044-0

DUBLINERS, James Joyce. Fifteen stories offer vivid, tightly focused observations of the lives of Dublin's poorer classes. At least one, "The Dead," is considered a masterpiece. Reprinted complete and unabridged from standard edition. 160pp. 5³⁄₁₆ x 8¼. 0-486-26870-5

THE LITTLE RED SCHOOLHOUSE, Eric Sloane. Harkening back to a time when the three Rs stood for reading, 'riting, and religion, Sloane's sketchbook explores the history of early American schools. Includes marvelous illustrations of one-room New England schoolhouses, desks, and benches. 48pp. 8¼ x 11. 0-486-45604-8

THE BOOK OF THE SACRED MAGIC OF ABRAMELIN THE MAGE, translated by S. MacGregor Mathers. Medieval manuscript of ceremonial magic. Basic document in Aleister Crowley, Golden Dawn groups. 268pp. 5⅜ x 8½. 0-486-23211-5

THE BATTLES THAT CHANGED HISTORY, Fletcher Pratt. Eminent historian profiles 16 crucial conflicts, ancient to modern, that changed the course of civilization. 352pp. 5⅜ x 8½. 0-486-41129-X

NEW RUSSIAN-ENGLISH AND ENGLISH-RUSSIAN DICTIONARY, M. A. O'Brien. This is a remarkably handy Russian dictionary, containing a surprising amount of information, including over 70,000 entries. 366pp. 4½ x 6⅛. 0-486-20208-9

NEW YORK IN THE FORTIES, Andreas Feininger. 162 brilliant photographs by the well-known photographer, formerly with *Life* magazine. Commuters, shoppers, Times Square at night, much else from city at its peak. Captions by John von Hartz. 181pp. 9¼ x 10¾. 0-486-23585-8

INDIAN SIGN LANGUAGE, William Tomkins. Over 525 signs developed by Sioux and other tribes. Written instructions and diagrams. Also 290 pictographs. 111pp. 6⅛ x 9¼. 0-486-22029-X

ANATOMY: A Complete Guide for Artists, Joseph Sheppard. A master of figure drawing shows artists how to render human anatomy convincingly. Over 460 illustrations. 224pp. 8⅜ x 11¼. 0-486-27279-6

MEDIEVAL CALLIGRAPHY: Its History and Technique, Marc Drogin. Spirited history, comprehensive instruction manual covers 13 styles (ca. 4th century through 15th). Excellent photographs; directions for duplicating medieval techniques with modern tools. 224pp. 8⅜ x 11¼. 0-486-26142-5

CATALOG OF DOVER BOOKS

DRIED FLOWERS: How to Prepare Them, Sarah Whitlock and Martha Rankin. Complete instructions on how to use silica gel, meal and borax, perlite aggregate, sand and borax, glycerine and water to create attractive permanent flower arrangements. 12 illustrations. 32pp. 5⅜ x 8½. 0-486-21802-3

EASY-TO-MAKE BIRD FEEDERS FOR WOODWORKERS, Scott D. Campbell. Detailed, simple-to-use guide for designing, constructing, caring for and using feeders. Text, illustrations for 12 classic and contemporary designs. 96pp. 5⅜ x 8½. 0-486-25847-5

THE COMPLETE BOOK OF BIRDHOUSE CONSTRUCTION FOR WOODWORKERS, Scott D. Campbell. Detailed instructions, illustrations, tables. Also data on bird habitat and instinct patterns. Bibliography. 3 tables. 63 illustrations in 15 figures. 48pp. 5¼ x 8½. 0-486-24407-5

SCOTTISH WONDER TALES FROM MYTH AND LEGEND, Donald A. Mackenzie. 16 lively tales tell of giants rumbling down mountainsides, of a magic wand that turns stone pillars into warriors, of gods and goddesses, evil hags, powerful forces and more. 240pp. 5⅜ x 8½. 0-486-29677-6

THE HISTORY OF UNDERCLOTHES, C. Willett Cunnington and Phyllis Cunnington. Fascinating, well-documented survey covering six centuries of English undergarments, enhanced with over 100 illustrations: 12th-century laced-up bodice, footed long drawers (1795), 19th-century bustles, 19th-century corsets for men, Victorian "bust improvers," much more. 272pp. 5⅝ x 8¼. 0-486-27124-2

FIRST FRENCH READER: A Beginner's Dual-Language Book, edited and translated by Stanley Appelbaum. This anthology introduces fifty legendary writers–Voltaire, Balzac, Baudelaire, Proust, more–through passages from The Red and the Black, Les Misérables, Madame Bovary, and other classics. Original French text plus English translation on facing pages. 240pp. 5⅜ x 8½. 0-486-46178-5

WILBUR AND ORVILLE: A Biography of the Wright Brothers, Fred Howard. Definitive, crisply written study tells the full story of the brothers' lives and work. A vividly written biography, unparalleled in scope and color, that also captures the spirit of an extraordinary era. 560pp. 6⅛ x 9¼. 0-486-40297-5

THE ARTS OF THE SAILOR: Knotting, Splicing and Ropework, Hervey Garrett Smith. Indispensable shipboard reference covers tools, basic knots and useful hitches; handsewing and canvas work, more. Over 100 illustrations. Delightful reading for sea lovers. 256pp. 5⅜ x 8½. 0-486-26440-8

FRANK LLOYD WRIGHT'S FALLINGWATER: The House and Its History, Second, Revised Edition, Donald Hoffmann. A total revision–both in text and illustrations–of the standard document on Fallingwater, the boldest, most personal architectural statement of Wright's mature years, updated with valuable new material from the recently opened Frank Lloyd Wright Archives. "Fascinating"–*The New York Times*. 116 illustrations. 128pp. 9¼ x 10¾. 0-486-27430-6

PHOTOGRAPHIC SKETCHBOOK OF THE CIVIL WAR, Alexander Gardner. 100 photos taken on field during the Civil War. Famous shots of Manassas Harper's Ferry, Lincoln, Richmond, slave pens, etc. 244pp. 10⅝ x 8¼. 0-486-22731-6

FIVE ACRES AND INDEPENDENCE, Maurice G. Kains. Great back-to-the-land classic explains basics of self-sufficient farming. The one book to get. 95 illustrations. 397pp. 5⅜ x 8½. 0-486-20974-1

CATALOG OF DOVER BOOKS

A MODERN HERBAL, Margaret Grieve. Much the fullest, most exact, most useful compilation of herbal material. Gigantic alphabetical encyclopedia, from aconite to zedoary, gives botanical information, medical properties, folklore, economic uses, much else. Indispensable to serious reader. 161 illustrations. 888pp. 6½ x 9¼. 2-vol. set. (Available in U.S. only.)   Vol. I: 0-486-22798-7   Vol. II: 0-486-22799-5

HIDDEN TREASURE MAZE BOOK, Dave Phillips. Solve 34 challenging mazes accompanied by heroic tales of adventure. Evil dragons, people-eating plants, blood-thirsty giants, many more dangerous adversaries lurk at every twist and turn. 34 mazes, stories, solutions. 48pp. 8¼ x 11.   0-486-24566-7

LETTERS OF W. A. MOZART, Wolfgang A. Mozart. Remarkable letters show bawdy wit, humor, imagination, musical insights, contemporary musical world; includes some letters from Leopold Mozart. 276pp. 5⅜ x 8½.   0-486-22859-2

BASIC PRINCIPLES OF CLASSICAL BALLET, Agrippina Vaganova. Great Russian theoretician, teacher explains methods for teaching classical ballet. 118 illustrations. 175pp. 5⅜ x 8½.   0-486-22036-2

THE JUMPING FROG, Mark Twain. Revenge edition. The original story of The Celebrated Jumping Frog of Calaveras County, a hapless French translation, and Twain's hilarious "retranslation" from the French. 12 illustrations. 66pp. 5⅜ x 8½.
0-486-22686-7

BEST REMEMBERED POEMS, Martin Gardner (ed.). The 126 poems in this superb collection of 19th- and 20th-century British and American verse range from Shelley's "To a Skylark" to the impassioned "Renascence" of Edna St. Vincent Millay and to Edward Lear's whimsical "The Owl and the Pussycat." 224pp. 5⅜ x 8½.
0-486-27165-X

COMPLETE SONNETS, William Shakespeare. Over 150 exquisite poems deal with love, friendship, the tyranny of time, beauty's evanescence, death and other themes in language of remarkable power, precision and beauty. Glossary of archaic terms. 80pp. 5³⁄₁₆ x 8¼.   0-486-26686-9

HISTORIC HOMES OF THE AMERICAN PRESIDENTS, Second, Revised Edition, Irvin Haas. A traveler's guide to American Presidential homes, most open to the public, depicting and describing homes occupied by every American President from George Washington to George Bush. With visiting hours, admission charges, travel routes. 175 photographs. Index. 160pp. 8¼ x 11.   0-486-26751-2

THE WIT AND HUMOR OF OSCAR WILDE, Alvin Redman (ed.). More than 1,000 ripostes, paradoxes, wisecracks: Work is the curse of the drinking classes; I can resist everything except temptation; etc. 258pp. 5⅜ x 8½.   0-486-20602-5

SHAKESPEARE LEXICON AND QUOTATION DICTIONARY, Alexander Schmidt. Full definitions, locations, shades of meaning in every word in plays and poems. More than 50,000 exact quotations. 1,485pp. 6½ x 9¼. 2-vol. set.
Vol. 1: 0-486-22726-X   Vol. 2: 0-486-22727-8

SELECTED POEMS, Emily Dickinson. Over 100 best-known, best-loved poems by one of America's foremost poets, reprinted from authoritative early editions. No comparable edition at this price. Index of first lines. 64pp. 5³⁄₁₆ x 8¼. 0-486-26466-1

THE INSIDIOUS DR. FU-MANCHU, Sax Rohmer. The first of the popular mystery series introduces a pair of English detectives to their archnemesis, the diabolical Dr. Fu-Manchu. Flavorful atmosphere, fast-paced action, and colorful characters enliven this classic of the genre. 208pp. 5³⁄₁₆ x 8¼.   0-486-29898-1

THE MALLEUS MALEFICARUM OF KRAMER AND SPRENGER, translated by Montague Summers. Full text of most important witchhunter's "bible," used by both Catholics and Protestants. 278pp. 6⅝ x 10.   0-486-22802-9

SPANISH STORIES/CUENTOS ESPAÑOLES: A Dual-Language Book, Angel Flores (ed.). Unique format offers 13 great stories in Spanish by Cervantes, Borges, others. Faithful English translations on facing pages. 352pp. 5⅜ x 8½.

0-486-25399-6

GARDEN CITY, LONG ISLAND, IN EARLY PHOTOGRAPHS, 1869–1919, Mildred H. Smith. Handsome treasury of 118 vintage pictures, accompanied by carefully researched captions, document the Garden City Hotel fire (1899), the Vanderbilt Cup Race (1908), the first airmail flight departing from the Nassau Boulevard Aerodrome (1911), and much more. 96pp. 8⅞ x 11¾.   0-486-40669-5

OLD QUEENS, N.Y., IN EARLY PHOTOGRAPHS, Vincent F. Seyfried and William Asadorian. Over 160 rare photographs of Maspeth, Jamaica, Jackson Heights, and other areas. Vintage views of DeWitt Clinton mansion, 1939 World's Fair and more. Captions. 192pp. 8⅞ x 11.   0-486-26358-4

CAPTURED BY THE INDIANS: 15 Firsthand Accounts, 1750-1870, Frederick Drimmer. Astounding true historical accounts of grisly torture, bloody conflicts, relentless pursuits, miraculous escapes and more, by people who lived to tell the tale. 384pp. 5⅜ x 8½.   0-486-24901-8

THE WORLD'S GREAT SPEECHES (Fourth Enlarged Edition), Lewis Copeland, Lawrence W. Lamm, and Stephen J. McKenna. Nearly 300 speeches provide public speakers with a wealth of updated quotes and inspiration—from Pericles' funeral oration and William Jennings Bryan's "Cross of Gold Speech" to Malcolm X's powerful words on the Black Revolution and Earl of Spenser's tribute to his sister, Diana, Princess of Wales. 944pp. 5⅜ x 8⅜.   0-486-40903-1

THE BOOK OF THE SWORD, Sir Richard F. Burton. Great Victorian scholar/adventurer's eloquent, erudite history of the "queen of weapons"—from prehistory to early Roman Empire. Evolution and development of early swords, variations (sabre, broadsword, cutlass, scimitar, etc.), much more. 336pp. 6⅛ x 9¼.

0-486-25434-8

AUTOBIOGRAPHY: The Story of My Experiments with Truth, Mohandas K. Gandhi. Boyhood, legal studies, purification, the growth of the Satyagraha (nonviolent protest) movement. Critical, inspiring work of the man responsible for the freedom of India. 480pp. 5⅜ x 8½. (Available in U.S. only.)   0-486-24593-4

CELTIC MYTHS AND LEGENDS, T. W. Rolleston. Masterful retelling of Irish and Welsh stories and tales. Cuchulain, King Arthur, Deirdre, the Grail, many more. First paperback edition. 58 full-page illustrations. 512pp. 5⅜ x 8½.   0-486-26507-2

THE PRINCIPLES OF PSYCHOLOGY, William James. Famous long course complete, unabridged. Stream of thought, time perception, memory, experimental methods; great work decades ahead of its time. 94 figures. 1,391pp. 5⅜ x 8½. 2-vol. set.
Vol. I: 0-486-20381-6   Vol. II: 0-486-20382-4

THE WORLD AS WILL AND REPRESENTATION, Arthur Schopenhauer. Definitive English translation of Schopenhauer's life work, correcting more than 1,000 errors, omissions in earlier translations. Translated by E. F. J. Payne. Total of 1,269pp. 5⅜ x 8½. 2-vol. set.   Vol. 1: 0-486-21761-2   Vol. 2: 0-486-21762-0

CATALOG OF DOVER BOOKS

MAGIC AND MYSTERY IN TIBET, Madame Alexandra David-Neel. Experiences among lamas, magicians, sages, sorcerers, Bonpa wizards. A true psychic discovery. 32 illustrations. 321pp. 5⅜ x 8½. (Available in U.S. only.) 0-486-22682-4

THE EGYPTIAN BOOK OF THE DEAD, E. A. Wallis Budge. Complete reproduction of Ani's papyrus, finest ever found. Full hieroglyphic text, interlinear transliteration, word-for-word translation, smooth translation. 533pp. 6½ x 9¼.
0-486-21866-X

HISTORIC COSTUME IN PICTURES, Braun & Schneider. Over 1,450 costumed figures in clearly detailed engravings–from dawn of civilization to end of 19th century. Captions. Many folk costumes. 256pp. 8⅜ x 11¾. 0-486-23150-X

MATHEMATICS FOR THE NONMATHEMATICIAN, Morris Kline. Detailed, college-level treatment of mathematics in cultural and historical context, with numerous exercises. Recommended Reading Lists. Tables. Numerous figures. 641pp. 5⅜ x 8½. 0-486-24823-2

PROBABILISTIC METHODS IN THE THEORY OF STRUCTURES, Isaac Elishakoff. Well-written introduction covers the elements of the theory of probability from two or more random variables, the reliability of such multivariable structures, the theory of random function, Monte Carlo methods of treating problems incapable of exact solution, and more. Examples. 502pp. 5⅜ x 8½. 0-486-40691-1

THE RIME OF THE ANCIENT MARINER, Gustave Doré, S. T. Coleridge. Doré's finest work; 34 plates capture moods, subtleties of poem. Flawless full-size reproductions printed on facing pages with authoritative text of poem. "Beautiful. Simply beautiful."–*Publisher's Weekly.* 77pp. 9¼ x 12. 0-486-22305-1

SCULPTURE: Principles and Practice, Louis Slobodkin. Step-by-step approach to clay, plaster, metals, stone; classical and modern. 253 drawings, photos. 255pp. 8⅛ x 11. 0-486-22960-2

THE INFLUENCE OF SEA POWER UPON HISTORY, 1660–1783, A. T. Mahan. Influential classic of naval history and tactics still used as text in war colleges. First paperback edition. 4 maps. 24 battle plans. 640pp. 5⅜ x 8½. 0-486-25509-3

THE STORY OF THE TITANIC AS TOLD BY ITS SURVIVORS, Jack Winocour (ed.). What it was really like. Panic, despair, shocking inefficiency, and a little heroism. More thrilling than any fictional account. 26 illustrations. 320pp. 5⅜ x 8½.
0-486-20610-6

ONE TWO THREE . . . INFINITY: Facts and Speculations of Science, George Gamow. Great physicist's fascinating, readable overview of contemporary science: number theory, relativity, fourth dimension, entropy, genes, atomic structure, much more. 128 illustrations. Index. 352pp. 5⅜ x 8½. 0-486-25664-2

DALÍ ON MODERN ART: The Cuckolds of Antiquated Modern Art, Salvador Dalí. Influential painter skewers modern art and its practitioners. Outrageous evaluations of Picasso, Cézanne, Turner, more. 15 renderings of paintings discussed. 44 calligraphic decorations by Dalí. 96pp. 5⅜ x 8½. (Available in U.S. only.) 0-486-29220-7

ANTIQUE PLAYING CARDS: A Pictorial History, Henry René D'Allemagne. Over 900 elaborate, decorative images from rare playing cards (14th–20th centuries): Bacchus, death, dancing dogs, hunting scenes, royal coats of arms, players cheating, much more. 96pp. 9¼ x 12¼. 0-486-29265-7

MAKING FURNITURE MASTERPIECES: 30 Projects with Measured Drawings, Franklin H. Gottshall. Step-by-step instructions, illustrations for constructing handsome, useful pieces, among them a Sheraton desk, Chippendale chair, Spanish desk, Queen Anne table and a William and Mary dressing mirror. 224pp. 8⅛ x 11¼.
0-486-29338-6

NORTH AMERICAN INDIAN DESIGNS FOR ARTISTS AND CRAFTSPEOPLE, Eva Wilson. Over 360 authentic copyright-free designs adapted from Navajo blankets, Hopi pottery, Sioux buffalo hides, more. Geometrics, symbolic figures, plant and animal motifs, etc. 128pp. 8⅜ x 11. (Not for sale in the United Kingdom.) 0-486-25341-4

THE FOSSIL BOOK: A Record of Prehistoric Life, Patricia V. Rich et al. Profusely illustrated definitive guide covers everything from single-celled organisms and dinosaurs to birds and mammals and the interplay between climate and man. Over 1,500 illustrations. 760pp. 7½ x 10⅛. 0-486-29371-8

VICTORIAN ARCHITECTURAL DETAILS: Designs for Over 700 Stairs, Mantels, Doors, Windows, Cornices, Porches, and Other Decorative Elements, A. J. Bicknell & Company. Everything from dormer windows and piazzas to balconies and gable ornaments. Also includes elevations and floor plans for handsome, private residences and commercial structures. 80pp. 9⅜ x 12¼. 0-486-44015-X

WESTERN ISLAMIC ARCHITECTURE: A Concise Introduction, John D. Hoag. Profusely illustrated critical appraisal compares and contrasts Islamic mosques and palaces—from Spain and Egypt to other areas in the Middle East. 139 illustrations. 128pp. 6 x 9. 0-486-43760-4

CHINESE ARCHITECTURE: A Pictorial History, Liang Ssu-ch'eng. More than 240 rare photographs and drawings depict temples, pagodas, tombs, bridges, and imperial palaces comprising much of China's architectural heritage. 152 halftones, 94 diagrams. 232pp. 10¾ x 9⅞. 0-486-43999-2

THE RENAISSANCE: Studies in Art and Poetry, Walter Pater. One of the most talked-about books of the 19th century, *The Renaissance* combines scholarship and philosophy in an innovative work of cultural criticism that examines the achievements of Botticelli, Leonardo, Michelangelo, and other artists. "The holy writ of beauty."—Oscar Wilde. 160pp. 5⅜ x 8½. 0-486-44025-7

A TREATISE ON PAINTING, Leonardo da Vinci. The great Renaissance artist's practical advice on drawing and painting techniques covers anatomy, perspective, composition, light and shadow, and color. A classic of art instruction, it features 48 drawings by Nicholas Poussin and Leon Battista Alberti. 192pp. 5⅜ x 8½. 0-486-44155-5

THE ESSENTIAL JEFFERSON, Thomas Jefferson, edited by John Dewey. This extraordinary primer offers a superb survey of Jeffersonian thought. It features writings on political and economic philosophy, morals and religion, intellectual freedom and progress, education, secession, slavery, and more. 176pp. 5⅜ x 8½. 0-486-46599-3

WASHINGTON IRVING'S RIP VAN WINKLE, Illustrated by Arthur Rackham. Lovely prints that established artist as a leading illustrator of the time and forever etched into the popular imagination a classic of Catskill lore. 51 full-color plates. 80pp. 8⅜ x 11. 0-486-44242-X

HENSCHE ON PAINTING, John W. Robichaux. Basic painting philosophy and methodology of a great teacher, as expounded in his famous classes and workshops on Cape Cod. 7 illustrations in color on covers. 80pp. 5⅜ x 8½. 0-486-43728-0

CATALOG OF DOVER BOOKS

LIGHT AND SHADE: A Classic Approach to Three-Dimensional Drawing, Mrs. Mary P. Merrifield. Handy reference clearly demonstrates principles of light and shade by revealing effects of common daylight, sunshine, and candle or artificial light on geometrical solids. 13 plates. 64pp. 5⅜ x 8½.   0-486-44143-1

ASTROLOGY AND ASTRONOMY: A Pictorial Archive of Signs and Symbols, Ernst and Johanna Lehner. Treasure trove of stories, lore, and myth, accompanied by more than 300 rare illustrations of planets, the Milky Way, signs of the zodiac, comets, meteors, and other astronomical phenomena. 192pp. 8⅜ x 11.
0-486-43981-X

JEWELRY MAKING: Techniques for Metal, Tim McCreight. Easy-to-follow instructions and carefully executed illustrations describe tools and techniques, use of gems and enamels, wire inlay, casting, and other topics. 72 line illustrations and diagrams. 176pp. 8¼ x 10⅞.   0-486-44043-5

MAKING BIRDHOUSES: Easy and Advanced Projects, Gladstone Califf. Easy-to-follow instructions include diagrams for everything from a one-room house for bluebirds to a forty-two-room structure for purple martins. 56 plates; 4 figures. 80pp. 8¾ x 6⅜.   0-486-44183-0

LITTLE BOOK OF LOG CABINS: How to Build and Furnish Them, William S. Wicks. Handy how-to manual, with instructions and illustrations for building cabins in the Adirondack style, fireplaces, stairways, furniture, beamed ceilings, and more. 102 line drawings. 96pp. 8¾ x 6⅜.   0-486-44259-4

THE SEASONS OF AMERICA PAST, Eric Sloane. From "sugaring time" and strawberry picking to Indian summer and fall harvest, a whole year's activities described in charming prose and enhanced with 79 of the author's own illustrations. 160pp. 8¼ x 11.   0-486-44220-9

THE METROPOLIS OF TOMORROW, Hugh Ferriss. Generous, prophetic vision of the metropolis of the future, as perceived in 1929. Powerful illustrations of towering structures, wide avenues, and rooftop parks—all features in many of today's modern cities. 59 illustrations. 144pp. 8¼ x 11.   0-486-43727-2

THE PATH TO ROME, Hilaire Belloc. This 1902 memoir abounds in lively vignettes from a vanished time, recounting a pilgrimage on foot across the Alps and Apennines in order to "see all Europe which the Christian Faith has saved." 77 of the author's original line drawings complement his sparkling prose. 272pp. 5⅜ x 8½.
0-486-44001-X

THE HISTORY OF RASSELAS: Prince of Abissinia, Samuel Johnson. Distinguished English writer attacks eighteenth-century optimism and man's unrealistic estimates of what life has to offer. 112pp. 5⅜ x 8½.   0-486-44094-X

A VOYAGE TO ARCTURUS, David Lindsay. A brilliant flight of pure fancy, where wild creatures crowd the fantastic landscape and demented torturers dominate victims with their bizarre mental powers. 272pp. 5⅜ x 8½.   0-486-44198-9

Paperbound unless otherwise indicated. Available at your book dealer, online at **www.doverpublications.com**, or by writing to Dept. GI, Dover Publications, Inc., 31 East 2nd Street, Mineola, NY 11501. For current price information or for free catalogs (please indicate field of interest), write to Dover Publications or log on to **www.doverpublications.com** and see every Dover book in print. Dover publishes more than 400 books each year on science, elementary and advanced mathematics, biology, music, art, literary history, social sciences, and other areas.